A
PRAYER
COLLECTIVE

FOUR GREAT CLASSICS ON PRAYER

Our Prayer DNA

How To Hear From God

The Seven Laws Of Asking & Receiving

The Eight Prayer Watches Of The Bible

A
PRAYER
COLLECTIVE

FOUR GREAT CLASSICS ON PRAYER

Our Prayer DNA

How To Hear From God

The Seven Laws Of Asking & Receiving

The Eight Prayer Watches Of The Bible

Sino & Kellie Agueze

XULON PRESS

Xulon Press
2301 Lucien Way #415
Maitland, FL 32751
407.339.4217
www.xulonpress.com

Unless otherwise indicated, Scripture quotations taken from
the King James Version (KJV) – *public domain*.

Printed in the United States of America.

ISBN-13: 978-1-5456-7963-0

TABLE OF CONTENTS

BOOK 1
OUR PRAYER DNA
THE PRAYER CULTURE OF THE WARRIOR NATION

BOOK 2
HOW TO HEAR FROM GOD
FLOWING IN GOD'S FREQUENCY

Book 3
The Seven Laws of Asking & Receiving
How to Pray & Receive Answers

Book 4
The Eight (8) Prayer Watches of the Bible
How to Develop a Stronger & Consistent Prayer Life

BOOK 1

Our Prayer DNA

The Prayer Culture of the Warrior Nation

CHAPTER 1

THE BIBLICAL PATTERN

THE BIBLICAL PATTERN REVEALED IN THE BOOK OF ACTS

It would be important, if not paramount, to begin by building a solid and thorough biblical foundation for New Testament prayer. This biblical pattern needs to be recaptured by today's church if we are expecting to have the same results. In Acts, we see a true move of the Spirit of God demonstrated through miracles, signs and wonders that brought entire cities to their knees. We vividly capture scenarios of whole-city conversions in a single day. Miracles of all types, including the raising of the dead are seen as a common phenomenon in the early church. And all the dramatic manifestations of the Spirit occurred as a result of prayer.

The early church had a clear prayer culture that stood head and shoulder above any other cause; including, the cause of evangelism. For the early church, evangelism was born out of prayer. Prayer led to a heavy and weighty manifestation of God's presence, which brought about the miracles, and which, in turn led to the salvation of multitudes of souls. Any true student of Acts, will quickly notice that miracles often always preceded conversions. Prayer

1

produced and kept the strong and mighty wind of God's Spirit blowing over them. And that strong wind continued to blow only as long as they kept praying. Acts 4:33 called it an explosion of "great grace." The Voice translation calls it extraordinary grace. We need to recapture this great grace at work in the church of our day. Recapturing the biblical pattern for prayer and recreating this prayer culture globally is the divine assignment of the "Warrior-Nation" family, and the M6:33 Movement.

We live and breathe prayer; and, exist to manifest Jesus in power. We are a people whose lives, like Anna in the Bible are given completely over to prayer as a way of life. We pray until the only challenge becomes our inability to stop praying.

The Book of Acts, which clearly depicts the church age, is filled with examples of a praying church woven all through it. It would be a grave mistake for us to ignore or fail to learn and to incorporate the prayer model into our lives, ministries and churches. This prayer model was revealed to us in Acts, and was practiced by the Apostles and disciples of the early church. This first church, the church in Acts is the divine model and anything less will not suffice. As already stated, it would be impossible to experience the same move of God without having the same prayer-culture or the same prayer-DNA that the early church had.

After the resurrection of Jesus from the dead, and right after the forty days He spent revealing this new order of His resurrection life to His disciples with irrefutable signs and wonders, He promised an outpouring of the Holy Spirit that would come upon all who believed, and it that would literally transform the course of human history forever. This outpouring of God's precious Holy Spirit would be the game changer. And it was to happen in a fashion, the likes which no man had never ever seen before. However,

2

the key to this outpouring wouldn't lie in the promise that Jesus made. The promise would only set into motion the legal premise necessary for the outpouring to happen. The key lay in one response—and that response was prayer. You'll noticed that 500 people heard the instruction to wait in Jerusalem for the outpouring of God's Spirit, but only 120 people responded. The 120 didn't have a passive response to Jesus' prophetic words. They didn't come up with excuses such as: "Well, if Jesus said something was going to happen in the next few days, then, that will suffice." They didn't go on a picnic or on a vacation. They didn't relinquish the responsibility of a prayer-response—instead they waited for the promise. They didn't believe that prophecies simply fulfilled themselves without the presence of an intercessor. What response did they have and what specific instruction did Jesus command them to have in response to His promise? Acts 1:14 shows us: "These all continued with one accord in prayer and supplication, with the women, and Mary the mother of Jesus, and with his brethren."

It was their prayer-response that brought about the outpouring.

The first and most important response in any situation should be to pray. Through united prayer, they birthed the literal fulfillment of God's promise, bringing it into a tangible manifestation of God's power. We, therefore can conclude that prophecies and promises are birthed into physical form by prayer. Prayer creates and causes divine momentum. Prayer gives birth to an inexplainable wind of God. Do you or your ministry or your church have this distinct and tangible wind of God's presence over it? And if not, why not? How many lives, ministries or churches are simply in a maintenance mode? The altars are dry and the pews are empty. They've explained away the miracles with empty philosophies of men. They've tiptoed around the presence, power and the gifts of the Holy Spirit and replaced them with dead programs and bondage protocols. Is God's wind blowing strong over you? The early church knew that the prayer-response to God's promise of an outpouring was the first and only right response. They knew that prophecies and promises fly on the wings of prayer. It was the continuity of prayer that birthed a God-movement and sustained it over time. A prayerless church is not a dying church; it's a dead church. However, God in His infinite mercy is pouring over us and our ministries again a fresh oil of prayer. Yes, a praying spirit is falling upon us in this hour—right now, in this kingdom moment. We are being clothed in a new mantle of prayer the likes of which we haven't seen or experienced in a long time. Can you feel it happening? Can you sense it already brewing? God has opened up a great and an effectual door for prayer in the heavens, but who is ready to step into it? Who is ready to launch into the depths of God's holy river and stay submerged?

F.F. Bosworth, in his book: *Christ the Healer* said this: "that when the church comes fully under the influence of the Holy Spirit, we shall see the same miracles that characterized the early church." With this, I wholeheartedly agree. May a true prayer revival start with me, in me and through me—go ahead and pray this prayer now: "Lord Jesus, let your fire on the altar of heart never burn out; let it ever be burning, Amen!"

> "These all continued with one accord in prayer and supplication, with the women, and Mary the mother of Jesus, and with his brethren" —Acts 1:14 KJV.

So, the outpouring happened in response to a united prayer, but It also continued as the result of ongoing united prayer. The first chapter of Acts reveals this as the scripture above shows it. I admire their dedication, consecration and commitment to prayer. It appears that they all prayed as if it all depended on prayer—here, we see the true attitude and posture of prayer.

We now jump to chapter 2, and see again the model church's dedication to prayer. The most fascinating thing about the prayer culture of the first church can be seen in the fact that every single believer had a strong prayer life. In other words, every believer was a prayer warrior in their own right. It wasn't a responsibility that was reserved for the few or for the elite or even for a special group of inter-cessors. It was everyone's divine calling—a shared respon-sibility among all the saints.

> "And they continued steadfastly in the apostles' doctrine and fellowship, in the breaking of bread, and in prayers"
> — Acts 2:42 NKJV.

The disciples continued steadfastly in prayers. These praying people wouldn't let up in prayer. There's an Old Testament scripture that reflects this attitude, and it's found in Isaiah 62:

> I have set watchmen upon thy walls, O Jerusalem, which shall never hold their peace day nor night: ye that make mention of the Lord, keep not silence, And give him no rest, till he establish, and till he make Jerusalem a praise in the earth — Isaiah 62:6-7 KJV.

A praying church never ceases to pray. They don't let up, cave in, slow down, take breaks or vacations in prayer. No! Rather, they keep the fire on the altar burning strong. Show me such a trained and persistent group of praying people, and I'll show you the secret to revival. Nothing keeps the wind of God blowing like a focused, determined and persistent group of praying people. O that today's church would forge this prayer habit—a people steadfastly committed to prayer. Pray we must, and we must pray as though all things in the kingdom depend on it, because they do. In Acts chapter 3, the scripture give us an insight into how the early church folks prayed.

> One day at three o'clock in the after-noon, a customary time for daily prayer, Peter and John walked to the temple — Acts 3:1 VOICE.

They had formed a customary time for daily prayer out of the habit of praying continually. At three o'clock every afternoon, the whole church came out to pray. And there's strong evidence to show that this was not the only prayer-watch that they regularly observed. Imagine how the early church prioritized prayer on a daily basis. And imagine further what would happen if we placed the same priority on prayer today. Recapturing this prayer culture is a must. We see again in Acts 10, where Cornelius, the Roman Centurion observed the 3pm prayer-watch coupled with fasting. Where did he learn about the 3pm customary time of prayer? I believe he learned it from the prayer culture of the early church. Peter, one of the chief apostles observed the sixth-hour prayer watch (the prayer watch at 12 noon) in Acts 10. There are eight prayer-watches that are mentioned in scripture. Four during the day and another four during the night. I believe that the early church observed several of these prayer watches. In the Acts 4, we see the power of their prayer life.

> And when they had prayed, the place was shaken where they were assembled together; and they were all filled with the Holy Ghost, and they spake the word of God with boldness — Acts 4:31 KJV.

Did you notice anything special about their prayer? They prayed to produce immediate impact—the place was shaken where they were assembled together, and they were all filled with the Holy Spirit, and they spoke God's word with boldness. What a New Testament revelation! What a paradigm for New Testament prayer. Why even pray if we won't pray that way? We come praying with a now-faith. Praying, believing that God will hear us in the moment, both then and now. Praying, believing that God will answer now. Praying, believing for immediate answers. He who comes to God must believe that He Is and that He is the rewarder of those who diligently seek Him — Hebrews 11:6. In prayer, we believe in the God that is, and not in the God that was or in the God that will be. And why? Because "He is" right here, right now. What He has been and what He'll be in the future have little to do with the moment in which we live now, so we must get into the moment and pray as if His answer will be coming now. I am neither living in the past or in the future; I am living right here, right now and I need God's intervention right away. This is the attitude of the prayer culture of the early church. Pray, expecting the answers now. True biblical faith is always now. We see this same effect of their prayer life when Paul and Silas prayed and sang praises to God. The very foundations of the prison were shaken and all the prison doors were opened — Acts 16:25-26. In the same way, Elijah prayed and immediately, God answered by fire. In fact, it was Prophet Elijah that mocked the prophets of Baal because their god was taking too much time to respond to their prayer.

> And it came to pass at noon, that Elijah mocked them, and said, Cry aloud: for he is a god; either he is talking, or he is pursuing, or he is in a journey, or peradventure he sleepeth, and must be awaked — 1 Kings 18:27 KJV.

Elijah felt that six hours was far too long a time for a living God to answer prayer. As far as he was concerned, the God he served — the God of Abraham, Isaac and Jacob answered him the moment he prayed. He served a God who always responded swiftly. After Solomon prayed in the dedication of the temple, God responded immediately with fire — 2 Chronicles 7:1. We need to change the paradigm that says it takes God forever to answer prayer. When we pray, let's pray believing. How long did it take God to hear Elijah's prayer? In one sentence of a heartfelt prayer, God answered by fire and turned the hearts of a nation back to Himself in a single moment of time.

In Acts chapter six, we see again the dedication the Apostles of Jesus gave to prayer. If all ministers in today's church understood this truth, we could turn the world upside down in no time. Aaron the High Priest and his sons were consecrated to the office of the priesthood for one sole purpose, and that was to minister to God — Ex. 30:20-22. This was true for the priests who served in the tabernacle of David. The early church in Acts lived out this same truth

8

in Acts 13:2. They gave themselves over to prayer, fasting, the ministry of the Word and ministering to God in praise and worship. These four elements of devotion consumed their very lives.

> But we will give ourselves continually
> to prayer, and to the ministry of the
> word — Acts 6:4 KJV.

Here again, we see the specific function that the early church leadership gave themselves to. They prioritized prayer above all else, and used the Word of God as wood to the fire to further fuel their prayer life. As a teen, it was the greatest joy of my friends and me to constantly meet for prayer. It was the highlight of our day; something we looked forward to with great anticipation. And when we prayed, it felt so good and resounded so powerfully. We prayed with great faith and believed for instantaneous answers to prayer, and God came through in a mighty way. May we all give ourselves to this high-priestly ministry. God, raise up a praying church with a praying leadership and a praying people. Blanket the church with a prayer mantle. Anoint her with fire from heaven, and baptize her with a spirit of prayer.

In Acts chapter twelve, the whole church gathered for prayer on behalf of Peter who had been locked up in a prison dungeon awaiting execution.

> All the time that Peter was under heavy
> guard in the jailhouse, the church
> prayed for him most strenuously —
> Acts 12:5 MSG.

> So Peter was kept in prison, but fervent and persistent prayer for him was being made to God by the church — Acts 12:5 AMP.

These scriptures help us see into the prayer lives of the early church. They show us that the early church prayed with such intensity and fervency that the place where they had prayed was shaken. They were used to praying earth-shaking prayers, and prayers that shook prison foundations. They meant business when they prayed, and their attitude showed that too. Their prayers brought dramatic manifestations of God down on the scene. A mighty angel came down from heaven and set Peter free from the prison and brought him out into the city. When we lose power in prayer, we start explaining away God's dramatic and supernatural manifestations. We explain away miracles, signs, wonders and angelic visitations. We explain away healings and deliverances. Lord, teach us how to pray again for a mighty outpouring of the Holy Spirit. This bunch had a unique grace that manifested God's very presence.

Examining the biblical pattern in Acts, it's obvious that prayer was their first and most prominent DNA. In other words, they had a notable and visible prayer culture. And that prayer culture led to them enjoying "grace-extraordinaire." Miracles were such a common phenomenon that Philip and Steven who were once chosen to serve tables were found performing miracles that turned entire cities to the Lord. There are twelve (12) distinct DNAs of the early church as follows:

"The DNA of Prayer; The DNA of His Presence; The DNA of Salvation; The DNA of Fellowship; The DNA of Discipleship; The DNA of Unity; The DNA of Consecration; The DNA of Miracles; The DNA of Selflessness; The DNA of Generosity; The DNA of Witnesses of His Resurrection; The DNA of Expansion."

And on top of that list, we have the prayer DNA. If God's church is ever to experience this level of grace in life and ministry as the early church did, then, we must develop the same or even a stronger prayer culture than they did. Like we often say it in the Warrior Nation, we live to pray and pray to live.

CHAPTER 2

THE ELIJAH PARADIGM

ELIJAH'S PRAYER LIFE REVEALED

Elijah was indeed a man of prayer. The Bible calls him a man who commanded the ear of God. However, there's so much more to this prophet's prayer life that will be revealed in this chapter. It's intriguing how the Bible leaves clues and hidden codes.

> Elijah was a man with human frailties, just like all of us, but he prayed and received supernatural answers. He actually shut the heavens over the land so there would be no rain for three and a half years! Then he prayed again and the skies opened up over the land so that the rain came again and produced the harvest — James 5:17-18 TPT.

The Epistles major on Elijah's prayer life more than any other subject. Although he was just as human as the rest of us, his prayer life set him apart. He prayed and received immediate answers. He had earned God's attention in his prayer life, so much so that people today still call on the

God of Elijah. What a reputation to have. And this praying prophet prayed that the heavens would not give rain for three and half years, and it didn't. And he prayed again, and the heavens gave rain. What a standing with God; what confidence and what a relationship! May God raise others with such grit. May we be known in this generation as men and women of prayer—yes, may we be known as a praying people and as a praying church.

> Even them will I bring to my holy mountain, and make them joyful in my house of prayer: their burnt offerings and their sacrifices shall be accepted upon mine altar; for mine house shall be called an house of prayer for all people — Isaiah 56:7 KJV.

It seems to me that the house of God should have a predominant trademark, and that distinct feature is prayer. And it's a house of prayer for all people. You'll notice also that prayer is the key to the harvesting of souls. That prayer produces a wind from God to thrust out laborers into the harvest field. Evangelism without prayer is a fruitless effort. However, evangelism fueled by prayer will always lead to an avalanche of souls saved.

In the Old Testament, the Bible gives us a glimpse into Elijah's prayer life.

> So Ahab went up to eat and to drink. And Elijah went up to the top of Carmel; and he cast himself down upon the earth, and put his face between his knees. And said to his servant, Go up now, look toward the sea. And he

> went up, and looked, and said, There is nothing. And he said, Go again seven times. And it came to pass at the seventh time, that he said, Behold, there ariseth a little cloud out of the sea, like a man's hand. And he said, Go up, say unto Ahab, Prepare thy chariot, and get thee down that the rain stop thee not —
> 1 Kings 18:42-44 KJV.

Elijah had the right response to the prophetic word that there would be a sound of abundance of rain. Ahab, the king, had the wrong response. While Elijah went up to the top of mount Carmel to pray, king Ahab went up to his palace to eat and drink. He was completely oblivious to the fact that every prophetic promise is driven into reality by prayer. In other words, you push prophecies and promises into physical reality through prayer. Elijah buried his face between his knees showing the ultimate force of focus. He cut-off all distractions and detractors and buried himself in God. And in this secret place of prayer, he would pray earnestly until the heavens responded. Did you know that when he asked his servant to go out to the Mediterranean Sea to check for any signs of rain, his servant came back and reported that he saw nothing. Upon which, Elijah asked him to go again and again seven times. At the seventh time, his servant saw a cloud the size of a man's hand, and this insignificant proof of a hand-size cloud was all that was needed to believe God for an outpouring of rain.

However, did you know that the distance from Mount Carmel to the Mediterranean Sea is a twelve mile walk one way or a twenty four mile round trip? And this, he had to do seven times. During all that time Elijah's servant walked back and forth from Mount Carmel to the Mediterranean

Sea, Elijah was praying. Conservatively, that would be about ten and a half hours, assuming that it would take the fastest walker forty-five minutes to walk twelve miles. This is an eye-opener into Elijah's prayer stamina. If we long to have the same results Elijah had, then we must have the same prayer power that he had. We must totally surrender our lives to prayer. We must persevere in prayer until the clouds break open with a mighty flood of God's glory. In other words, we must become a people given to prayer. We would see that this dedication to prayer in the life of all, both male and female, used greatly by God. If there's one need for freedom, it is the freedom to spend quantities of quality times in the presence of God. Herein lies the flow of fresh oil; herein lies power to cause changes. I am totally convinced that Elijah's prayer life—his life of communion with God was the secret to his miraculous life. We see the same paradigm in Enoch's life. The Bible tells us that Enoch had an unbroken habitual fellowship with God for 300 years. Imagine that! Three hundred years of prayer rising constantly to God like incense. What a tremendous deposit in his bank of glory from which he made eternal withdrawals. Revival is predicated upon prayer deposits. Elijah prayed and persevered in prayer until the heavens opened. We, too, must persevere until we prevail in prayer. May a holy prayer mantle filled with flames of fire from the altar of God fall like a blanket on the Warrior Nation Family. Prayer indeed is our oxygen. We live and breathe prayer.

"If the clouds are full of rain, they empty themselves upon the earth" — Ecclesiastes 11:3 KJV.

Making prayer deposits into God's glory bank is indispensable to revival. We cannot make withdrawals without

15

first making deposits. The outpouring we see in the Book of the Acts of the Apostles came from a praying generation of people who made large sums of prayer deposits into the glory-bank of heaven. The clouds of glory must be filled with rain in its gaseous form. Our prayers like incense must rise up and fill the clouds of glory. The goal is to keep the clouds full of rain. They empty themselves upon the earth only when they are full. And this is our prayer mandate and our prayer mission. We will achieve this by observing the eight (8) prayer watches of the Bible. Elijah prayed until the heavens gave her rain.

> Who can number the clouds in wisdom? or who can stay the bottles of heaven?—Job 38:37 KJV.

The scriptures call the clouds, the bottles of heaven. And when they are full of rain, He flips them over to empty them out. In Genesis, it rained non-stop for forty days and forty nights. Here, the windows of heaven were opened, and the clouds released her rain upon the earth, flooding it. As a ministry, we are praying for another flood of God's Spirit to envelop the earth again, leading to the salvation of entire nations —Revelation 21:24. Can we dare God to once again pour out His Spirit to cover the earth as the waters cover the sea? Yes, I know we can, and we should. Observing the prayer watches would be highly instrumental in birthing and sustaining a move of God. As a ministry, prayer, first and foremost drives all that we do. Prayer is the root, and soul winning is the fruit. If we keep these two things in front of us, and we will surely succeed.

CHAPTER 3

THE DANIEL PARADIGM

HOW PRAYER KEPT HIM ON THE CUTTING EDGE

D aniel has always been an interesting character for me in the Bible. I've admired him greatly as one of the most important personalities in all scripture. He was a man who deeply walked with God. A man of deep revelation of the scriptures. He is believed to have formed the school of the magi's. He was a man whose life impressed both God and all the angels in heaven. He was a man of principle, character and integrity. He was above all, a man of prayer. Without a doubt, prayer was the foundation to his unending and enduring life of success. He had no rivals. He was in a class by himself. He prayed until everyone in Persia knew about it. Those in the corridors of power were fully aware of his commitment to prayer, which was non-negotiable and uncompromising. Here, he drew the line. Others around him valued his prayer life because of the value he placed on it. May others value your prayer time as well. May nothing in this world take the place of prayer in your life. Make up your mind that you're not going to cut corners in this area of your life. Take a firm stand and make your prayer life explosive.

When Daniel learned that the decree had been signed and posted, he continued to pray just as he had always done. His house had windows in the upstairs that opened toward Jerusalem. Three times a day he knelt there in prayer, thanking and praising his God — Daniel 6:10 MSG.

Daniel, who literally administered the affairs of the state as a prime minister, made prayer a far more important priority than his political responsibilities. In fact, his primary focus was praying to God, and everything else naturally flowed out of it. If you keep the root healthy and strong, the fruit will naturally be healthy and strong. Each day, three times a day, he would travel between work and home to pray. He had forged it into a habit. He prayed morning, afternoon and evening each and every day, and everyone in the nation knew it. Prayer was truly the source of his power and success. It was the secret means of keeping his creative juices flowing. Daniel was so in tune with God that the heavens were opened up to him, giving him all the answers to the problems confronting his nation. He was always at the cutting edge of information, both divine and natural. His prayer life gave him the edge over his contemporaries in every instance.

Darius reorganized his kingdom. He appointed one hundred twenty governors to administer all the parts of his realm. Over them were three vice-regents, one of whom was Daniel. The governors reported to the vice-regents, who made sure that everything

> was in order for the king. But Daniel,
> brimming with spirit and intelligence,
> so completely outclassed the other
> vice-regents and governors that the
> king decided to put him in charge of
> the whole kingdom — Daniel 6:1 MSG.

That's what your prayer life is going to do for you. It releases a flow of fresh oil into your life. It activates the unused places of your mind while maximizing all your creative juices. And creativity powerfully affects productivity. Fresh oil makes your mind a super mind—an intelligentsia of a higher order. God's presence keeps you in the know, always. It keeps you current. It keeps you in the now. Prayer keeps you flowing in God's frequency, and therefore, attuned to His will.

Daniel was brimming with spirit and intelligence and constantly outclassed all of his peers. His wisdom was described as the wisdom of the gods. Warrior Nation, this is where God wants us all to function from in our daily lives. He wants us to rule the day as well as the night, and to take full command of life. We take command of life by taking command of light.

> When his candle shined upon my head,
> and when by his light I walked through
> darkness; As I was in the days of my
> youth, when the secret of God was
> upon my tabernacle — Job 29:3-4 KJV.

Prayer adjusts and fine-tunes your spirit. It places your inner-man in command. It puts your spirit in the place of victory. And the state of your spirit determines the state of your mind. Your mind, like a sponge, absorbs all the

19

workings of God in your born-again spirit. In other words, God thinks through the vessel of your mind. And Daniel's mind was constantly under the influence of God's Spirit and his approach to life was an amazement to everyone around him.

> God gave these four young men knowledge and skill in both books and life. In addition, Daniel was gifted in understanding all sorts of visions and dreams. At the end of the time set by the king for their training, the head of the royal staff brought them in to Nebuchadnezzar. When the king interviewed them, he found them far superior to all the other young men. None were a match for Daniel, Hananiah, Mishael, and Azariah. And so they took their place in the king's service. Whenever the king consulted them on anything, on books or on life, he found them ten times better than all the magicians and enchanters in his kingdom put together —Daniel 1:17-19 MSG.

The more they pressed into a deeper prayer life with God, the more they tapped into a world of wisdom beyond the natural realm—Job 28:12-22. They had access to the secrets of unrivaled success. They revealed and interpreted the king's dreams and provided answers to complex problems. They were ten times better than the best. And all because they maintained an unbroken habitual communion with God. They kept Holy Ghost oil flowing fresh multiple times a day. And so should we, constantly flowing in the frequency of God. Our prayer lives ought to be powerful; and all of hell should tremble when we pray. No more cute and calculated prayers! We pray from the heart as if our lives depended on it—and it just may. Let's get into the habit of praying multiple times a day. Let's take advantage of every opportunity to pray. Don't just make the day count; make it "prayer-count." Make many prayer deposits into your glory-bank. It's time to cause it to rain; and not just for forty days and nights, but for the next forty years. Join us and let's unreservedly commit ourselves to a life of prayer. Who wouldn't want to live in the orbit of God's glory? Who wouldn't want to live under the manifest presence of God? Who wouldn't long for a constant flow of fresh oil? Who wouldn't want to be attuned to God's voice around the clock? Is it possible? Yes, it is! Is it doable? Absolutely yes, it is!

Then we can use all our time to pray and to teach the word of God" — Acts 6:4 ERV.

But we will [continue to] devote ourselves [steadfastly] to prayer and to the ministry of the word" — Acts 6:4 AMP.

Then we shall devote ourselves whole-heartedly to prayer and the ministry of the Word" — Acts 6:1 PHILLIPS.

Meanwhile, we'll stick to our assigned tasks of prayer and speaking God's Word" — Acts 6:1 MSG.

So we can maintain our focus on praying and serving—not meals—but the message — Acts 6:4 VOICE.

❧CHAPTER 4❧

THE MOSES PARADIGM

EIGHTY DAYS IN GOD'S PRESENCE

Moses had an unusual relationship with God. He related to God as a man would to another human being—as one would to a best friend. He was always in communion with God, and constantly lived in the frequency of God. And if Moses, an old covenant man, lived such a remarkable life with God, how much more should the "man in Christ" live such an extraordinary life—a life that should literally turn the world upside down? Who's ready to live this kind of a life in Christ? Who's ready to live in such fullness of life in the Spirit? Who's ready to live a life where God is more real to you than a best friend? Hearing God's voice is going to become far more natural to us in this generation—far more natural than that of a parent to a child. Who's ready to tap into this dimension of the spirit and dance in the orbit of a move of God? It's time to enter into this power zone—a place far greater than Eden where the first Adam lived before the fall. And in this place, we will live above the clouds where there's no consciousness of sickness and disease; where there's no consciousness of darkness; and, where there's no consciousness of lack or the consciousness of all that occurred under the fall. Warrior Nation, God has called us to live in our natural habitat, seated with the Lord of glory in heavenly places far superior to all principality and power. And in the name of Jesus Christ of Nazareth, we are already on our way to living in this realm. This realm of God's Spirit is not a strange place. Rather, it is the home of our born-again spirits. Can anyone hear the call home? It's the call of the Spirit, and He is calling us to become conscious of our original abode. Moses is known as a man who was face-to-face with God.

> And there arose not a prophet since in Israel like unto Moses, whom the Lord knew face to face, In all the signs and the wonders, which the Lord sent him to do in the land of Egypt to Pharaoh, and to all his servants, and to all his land
> — Deuteronomy 34:10-11 KJV.

Moses had a very unique relationship with God. He became a man who knew God face-to-face. In other words, he had a face-to face relationship with God.

> "So the Lord spoke to Moses face to face, as a man speaks to his friend ..."
> Exodus 33:11 NKJV.

Moses would often meet with God either at the tent of meeting or on Mount Sinai. Here, God would come down shrouded in the cloud of glory and speak with Moses mouth to mouth. They both had audible conversations — a dialogue so to speak. This method of communication became Moses' norm. However, the more frequent their intimate fellowship, the more Moses became transformed by God's

23

presence. Moses had a vital, living relationship with God. That fellowship was revealed in a face-to-face, mouth-to-mouth and heart-to-heart constant flow of conversation between the two of them. We should yearn for this type of fellowship, living in the constant flow of an unbreakable union with God. God in us and us in God, inseparably and vitally connected in a mystical union. Moses shared in the life of God. He partook of God's divine presence, and it rubbed off on Him. That fresh oil of God's presence saturated his very being—every single fiber of his being. It literally suspended the aging gene his natural human life.

> And he said, Hear now my words: If there be a prophet among you, I the Lord will make myself known unto him in a vision, and will speak unto him in a dream. My servant Moses is not so, who is faithful in all mine house. With him will I speak mouth to mouth, even apparently, and not in dark speeches; and the similitude of the Lord shall he behold: wherefore then were ye not afraid to speak against my servant Moses? Numbers 12:6-8 KJV.

Even God boasted about His personal relationship with Moses to both Aaron and Miriam, the siblings of Moses. It seems to be suggesting that there are two levels on which God may choose to reveal Himself to someone. One method is an indirect manifestation of Himself through a medium, such as: a dream, a vision, a person, promptings, prophecies or impressions and or other divine signals. The other way is a direct and open manifestation of Himself even to the point of beholding His very manifest form, which requires no means or medium whatever. I'm convinced that we've now entered a phase where we will be able to behold the beauty of God in His tangible form. I call this a face-to-face fellowship with God—the same kind of fellowship Adam enjoyed with God. He heard the sound of God's voice in the cool of the day. God's voice is alive and powerful, able to call things into being with a single word. Jesus, the second and last Adam said, "I only do what I see my Father do." This is the mystery behind the meaning of life itself. The truth is that life is a person, and that person is Jesus, and He is the focus of both heaven and earth. Paul, the apostle said that he has counted all other things as a dung compared to the joy of knowing Jesus. May this become our sincere cry: to know Him is life eternal — John 17:3. Cast away now all encumbrances and the complexities of life, and get back to the one thing that really matters: "knowing Him, and to making Him known." I'm literally talking about a face-to-face fellowship with God. I can't say this enough: that all true transformation comes as the result of an encounter with the person, the presence and the power of Jesus. Do you know what we need? We need encounters with the person of Jesus. That's it right there—it's the biggest sweepstakes win we could ever imagine.

CHAPTER 5

THE PAUL PARADIGM

A TRUE MAN OF ABUNDANCE OF REVELATIONS

P aul the Apostle is arguably, the greatest apostle that ever lived to date. Most ignore or are unaware of his life of prayer. He once said that he prayed in tongues more than the entire church combined — 1 Corinthians 14:18. Almost all the Epistles written by him begin with unceasing, fervent prayer for the saints. Paul spent so many days and nights in prayer. In I Thessalonians, he admonishes us to pray without ceasing. In Ephesians, he tells us to pray with all manner of prayer. In Colossians, he prayed that the church would be filled with the exact knowledge of God's will. And at the end of his life, he never ceased, but longingly cried out to know Jesus and the power of His resurrection. Because of that intimate fellowship with God, he lived under an open heaven, and had an unlimited abundance of the revelations by God's Spirit. His human spirit could ascend to the third heaven and hear things that were unlawful for mortal men to hear. He was given kingdom secrets only meant for the world to come. His soul capacity was so huge that God decided to use him to write two-thirds of the New Testament. Paul impacted many nations with the gospel of Jesus Christ without any type of media platform, which obviously didn't exist during his time. He was without doubt, a man of prayer.

> My little children, of whom I travail in
> birth again until Christ be formed in you
> — Galatians 4:19 KJV.

Paul travailed in prayer not only for the salvation of men's souls, but also for their discipleship in the faith. Children are begotten by travailing prayers, and kept in the faith the same way. In Mississippi for instance, there is a huge revolving door among the African American churches. The cure? Give birth to your own spiritual children through prayer and they'll stay. Paul prayed and preached, and that's the summary of his life and ministry. Jesus, our Savior and Lord, summarized His ministry as follows: "I do what I see the Father do; and, I say what I hear the Father say." And that happened because of their fellowship-bond. In God's Word, Paul encourages us to enjoy rich fellowship with God in His Word.

> "Let the word of Christ dwell in you richly
> in all wisdom ... " Colossians 3:16 KJV.

And he tells us to abide in the fellowship of the Spirit of God — 2 Corinthians 13:14. In that amazing communion with God, Paul the Apostle, grew beyond human limits in his faith, and in his understanding of the gospel of Jesus Christ. He had many encounters with God that helped him thrive both in his personal life and ministry. The heavens entrusted him with the gospel of the glorious grace of our Lord Jesus Christ. All this and so much more, came as a result of his prayer life.

☙ CHAPTER 6 ❧

THE JESUS PARADIGM

THE ULTIMATE PRAYER WARRIOR

Jesus is the ultimate prayer warrior. Everything about Him was centered on a unique communion with His Father. He knew His Father, and that knowledge of His Father was the secret behind His success. I noticed that nothing, no matter how important or expedient, could distract Him from the presence of His Father. Often, in the immediate aftermath of healing multitudes of people, He would break away from the crowds to seek His Father's presence. Although He was God's Son, and also, anointed without measure, He ardently sought after God early, before the breaking of the day. It seemed He never made a single move without the Father's approval.

> And at even, when the sun did set, they brought unto him all that were diseased, and them that were possessed with devils. And all the city was gathered together at the door. And he healed many that were sick of divers diseases, and cast out many devils; and suffered not the devils to speak, because they

> knew him. And in the morning, rising up
> a great while before day, he went out,
> and departed into a solitary place, and
> there prayed—Mark 1:32-35 KJV.

Jesus prayed—so much so that His own disciples marveled at His prayer life. This sweet fellowship with God was the oxygen of His life, and the very force behind His exploits. His day started with strange and unusual encounters with God. Through prayer encounters, He'd download the full blueprint of all that the Father had planned for Him to accomplish that day. He said, "I only do what I see the Father do." He flowed in sync and in step with the Father. May we too have our greatest delight in the Father's presence. How did we complicate Christianity to the complex thing it's become today? It's actually very simple. It's all about face-to-face fellowship with God. It's taking daily delight in God's presence. It includes enjoying gazing at the beauty of God. That's it. This sweet fellowship is the high of all highs. In this place, sacrifices become joys; sufferings become pleasures; and dying for His cause defines the true meaning of living. The most important thing the disciples asked was that He would train them to pray like He prayed. At the Mount of Olives, Jesus prayed until His whole countenance lit up like the sun with the glory of God. His body became luminous with the glory of their communion.

> As he prayed, his face began to glow
> until it was a blinding glory streaming
> from him. His entire body was illumi-
> nated with a radiant glory. His bright-
> ness became so intense that it made
> his clothing blinding white, like multiple
> flashes of lightning — Luke 9:29 TPT.

29

That prayer was rooted in a deep communion of the heart that no mortal mind can imagine. His prayer life brought His entire being into perfect harmony with God. The light from His Father illuminated His whole being, manifesting through His human body. We too should have His life at work in us willing and doing of His great pleasure. Let His life be made manifest in our mortal bodies — 2 Corinthians 4:10-12. May we also have a prayer life that produces immediate results. May we all be called back to the place of prayer—a place of His presence that nothing in this world or the next can ever compete with. May seeking financial freedom be for the sake of spending quantities of quality times with God. May we pray until the heavens transform us from the inside out. I declare to myself: "Sino, pray until you're completely transformed from the inside out! Pray Sino, until all of you becomes cut up in a vortex of prayer. Pray until all the cells in both spirit and body cannot cease from praying. In that mystic union with Christ, we're forever one with Him in spirit, inseparably united as one flesh. And in this oneness, spirit to spirit, the deep calls to deep—hallelujah! Here, we live in unbroken, habitual communion with God.

At the end of His life, the night before He was crucified, Jesus prayed in Gethsemane until His skin sweated blood. The weight of the sins of the world was being placed upon His soul that awful night. In much agony, He travailed in prayer to the point of death. He won that battle of the cross and won the victor's crown that very night in prayer. Through prayer the powers of hell were vanquished, and the finished work of Christ was accomplished that night. All that followed afterwards was simply to fulfill all righteousness.

❧ CHAPTER 7 ❧

DEFINING OUR
PRAYER CULTURE

THE SEVEN CHARACTERISTICS OF OUR
PRAYER CULTURE

L et's define our prayer culture. Our prayer culture can be defined by the following characteristics:

1. INTIMACY

Defining the word 'intimacy', we mean a connectivity with God that has no bounds or limits. It's a divine romance in the height, depth, length and width of God's love. Intimacy means to enjoy the overflow of God's grace, much like a constant drinking from waters from near a deeply-rooted tree. This intimacy with God is the secret to discovering the beauty of life the way God intended. Hear this like your life depended on it: if you miss it here, you've missed it everywhere else. How often we all complicate life, making things far more complex than God intended them to be. Can we all go back to what matters—the simplicity of faith in the Christ who died to save us from sin?

What if I were to tell you that when it all comes down to it, only one thing counts—only one thing really matters. Everything else is secondary. However, in many of our lives, we've become encumbered by much unnecessary baggage. Things that have absolutely nothing to do with our destinies, and things that have nothing to do with the true meaning of life. We've gotten so distracted and derailed along the way with the mundane cares of this life. Our lives have become so clogged that it obstructed the river of life from flowing within us. Yes, we've gotten busy doing all the right things in the wrong places at the wrong time. But I believe that all of that can change if we seek first His kingdom and His righteousness.

> As they continued their travel, Jesus entered a village. A woman by the name of Martha welcomed him and made him feel quite at home. She had a sister, Mary, who sat before the Master, hanging on every word he said. But Martha was pulled away by all she had to do in the kitchen. Later, she stepped in, interrupting them. "Master, don't you care that my sister has abandoned the kitchen to me? Tell her to lend me a hand." The Master said, "Martha, dear Martha, you're fussing far too much and getting yourself worked up over nothing. One thing only is essential, and Mary has chosen it—it's the main course, and won't be taken from her."
> Luke 10:38, 41 MSG.

How could something as important as preparing a meal be distracting? Kitchen duties which are essential to our physical sustenance pale in comparison to feasting at the feet of Jesus. This is the one thing that matters: enjoying Jesus as our ultimate best friend. That's the summary of all our existence. This was the secret to Enoch's extraordinary life with God.

> Enoch walked [in habitual fellowship] with God three hundred years after the birth of Methuselah and had other sons and daughters. So all the days of Enoch were three hundred and sixty-five years. And [in reverent fear and obedience] Enoch walked with God; and he was not [found among men], because God took him [away to be home with Him] — Genesis 5:22-24 AMP.

Does this mean that there are no other important things to do in this life? Of course not! But all other causes, no matter how important, are simply a by-product of this one vital thing. Everything else flows out of this one source. And without that source, there's no resource from which to draw. Without roots, there is no fruit. We're chasing fruits without roots—that's what a life in Christ is like without fellowship. And that kind of a life is pretty exhausting. In both extraordinary or ordinary tasks of life, it should be our goal to enjoy Jesus as a person, but even more as a dear friend and confidante. In fact, that should be our only goal! And we can do this, no matter what other responsibilities we face. This is the actual calling both you and I have been designed to do.

God is faithful, by whom you were called
into the fellowship of His Son, Jesus
Christ our Lord — 1 Corinthians 1:9 NKJV.

I've come to believe that many of us have actually put
the cart before the horse. And that's exactly like being a fish
out of water. It's impossible, impractical and self-defeating.
Anyone felt like that lately? We've embraced everything
else but the one thing that matters—the only thing, really!
Can't get no power without a power source. I think it's high
time we got back to being plugged into our power source,
and let the current of His life flow uninhibited into ours.

2. JEALOUSY

The disciples were astounded, but
they remembered that the Hebrew
Scriptures said, "Jealous devotion for God's house consumes me."
John 2:17 VOICE.

This is the second characteristic of our prayer culture.
Not jealousy in the ordinary sense, but jealousy over the
honor and glory of God that drives us to pray. We who are
passionately in love with Him are extremely jealous for the
honor of His name. We badly want to see Jesus lifted up
so that all men may see and seek Him with all their hearts,
souls and minds. And we will not stop seeking it, nor hold
our peace until Jerusalem becomes a praise in the earth.

O God, how long shall the adversary
reproach? shall the enemy blaspheme
thy name for ever? Psalm 74:10 KJV.

We feel like King David felt when Goliath blasphemed God in the land of Israel. And in all the land of Israel, no one stood up to defend the name of God, except him. David felt His God was being insulted by the Philistine giant, and was let down, even betrayed, by Israel. When he finally decided to defend God's honor, he was criticized and humiliated by his people and loudly reprimanded by his older brothers. In spite of that overwhelming opposition, he faced impossible odds, believed God, and defended His honor against Goliath, ultimately winning a stunning victory for God and Israel. Today, I feel exactly the same way. The insatiable need to manifest Jesus to a dying world and a lukewarm church will never cease as long as I have breath inside me. The hunger to reveal Him to this generation in signs, wonders and miracles is literally eating me up from the inside out. I can't stand to see Him dishonored. How can we not have a rebirthing of the Book of the Acts of the Apostles in our generation? How is that thought impossible? Why would any of us choose to spend another day without seeing a powerful and unarguably supernatural move of God? What would be the benefit of that? May God's fiery jealousy burn seven times hotter on the altar of our hearts. In a generation where many are losing the knowledge and the fear of God, nothing less than a sweeping move of God will suffice to turn things around. Let the wind of God blow and change everything!

3. AGGRESSION

By aggression, I mean spiritual aggression. It manifests as aggressively pursuing God in prayer, seeking to touch His very heart with our petitions. It's a prayer posture we take on with a victor's mentality, and it shows in our very actions. You remember the same faith-action God was expecting to witness from the children of Israel on the night of their deliverance from the house of bondage? It may surprise us to discover that they were acting like they didn't want out of Egypt—Exodus <u>12:12-13</u>. In prayer, we come with an all-conquering attitude. We come with a faith attitude, like the widow woman in Luke eighteen, who never gave up or caved in until she got what she wanted. In Acts four, the disciples prayed with such certainty that the very grounds shook beneath their feet. Jesus prayed at Lazarus' grave site with no doubt that he was going to rise from the dead.

> From the time of John the Baptizer until now, the kingdom of heaven has been forcefully advancing, and forceful people have been seizing it. Matthew 11:12 GW.

> From the moment John stepped onto the scene until now, the realm of heaven's kingdom is bursting forth, and passionate people have taken hold of its power. Matthew 11:12 TPT

There's an aggression in the spirit that God wants us to command. It's a prayer aggression where we take a stand, arguing our God-given legal rights. Any encroachment or trespass on our legal boundaries demands the right and godly response from deep inside us, until we get the answers we need. It requires the roar of the lion sending the message that the king has arrived and every enemy must back down and bow to the will of the king. This attitude in prayer is necessary in contending for the lost souls of our families and loved ones. It's needed when your mind and your body has been violated with sicknesses and diseases. It's needed when a ceiling placed over your progress in life must be broken once and for all. Being spiritually aggressive is part of our prayer culture. It's not something we create or rev up in the flesh—rather it's all motivated by the Holy Spirit who lays the burden on our hearts, and inspires us to fervently pray and seek Him from the inside out. It is the war-dance of the Holy Ghost rumbling in our inner-man until we see answers manifest right here, right now.

4. INSTANT RESULTS

The fourth characteristic of our prayer culture is having instant results and answers to prayer.

> Therefore I say unto you, What things soever ye desire, when ye pray, believe that ye receive them, and ye shall have them — Mark 11:24 KJV.

I am not too sure how many of us understand this scripture. Let's see it again in Matthew.

> And all things, whatsoever ye shall ask in prayer, believing, ye shall receive. Matthew 21:22 KJV.

This prayer of faith demands that once prayer is offered you believe, and believing that you receive the answer to the prayer that you've offered. In other words, pray believing that you receive at the instant of prayer. We must come praying, and believing that He is — Hebrews 11:6. We

37

don't pray believing that He was or will be, as if it's in doubt, that maybe He won't move on our behalf. What's the use of praying if you're not believing God for the answer? We shouldn't pray unless we pray with the attitude that God will answer the moment we pray. As previously stated, Prophet Elijah considered six hours too long a time for God to answer prayer. He openly mocked all the gods of baal for taking that long to hear the miserable cries of his prophets. Without faith that He will move in that moment, it's impossible to please God. Why? Because he who comes to God (in prayer) must believe that He is — He is a right-now God. You have it when you believe that you receive. If we prayed like this, we would without fail have instant answers to our prayers. This is something we need to aspire to, and work on, because that's the way they prayed and got results in the Book of Acts.

5. Manifestations

Our fervent prayers come with proofs. When Jesus prayed, undeniable proofs inevitably followed. God is in the business of confirming the word of His messengers with signs following — Mark 16:20. Scriptures consistently point out that the kingdom of God is not in word only, but also in power — 1 Corinthians 4:20; 1 Thessalonians 1:5; Romans 15:18-19; Acts 9:34-35; Acts 9:36-42. It's the only biblical pattern of winning whole cities for Christ that I know of. Manifestations manifest Him on the scene and confirm the spoken words. Jesus spoke of this:

> Believe me that I am in the Father, and the Father in me: or else believe me for the very works' sake — John 14:11 KJV.

His works (proofs, demonstrations, manifestations) reveal Him to the world. It shows that He is a real living person walking and working among the people in the earth today. Without signs, the gospel of the Lord Jesus would not go far. Our prayers must command signs.

> And when they heard that, they lifted up their voice to God with one accord, and said, Lord, thou art God, which hast made heaven, and earth, and the sea, and all that in them is:
>
> And now, Lord, behold their threatenings: and grant unto thy servants, that with all boldness they may speak thy word. By stretching forth thine hand to heal; and that signs and wonders may be done by the name of thy holy child Jesus.
>
> And when they had prayed, the place was shaken where they were assembled together; and they were all filled with the Holy Ghost, and they spake the word of God with boldness.
>
> And with great power gave the apostles witness of the resurrection of the Lord Jesus: and great grace was upon them all — Acts 4:24,29-31,33 KJV.

What happened after they prayed that God would stretch His hand through their hands to heal the sick? The place was shaken, they were all re-filled with the Holy Spirit,

39

spake God's Word with boldness, and gave irrefutable witness of the resurrection of Christ from the dead.

6. Lock-ins

What do we mean by "lock-ins"? We mean the habit of taking half a day or whole days and spending them exclusively in the presence of God, and often in a fast. May God help us to see the importance of this: the spending of whole days in God's presence away from the hustle and bustle of life. These journeys in God must become more regular. Part of the reason why I am a huge proponent of financial freedom is the freedom to buy time so that you and I can spend it in His presence. This ancient landmark needs to be restored in the church if we are ever going to see mighty moves of God in the earth. In these lock-ins we spend time with the "Living Word." We sit at the feet of the Holy Spirit to learn all that is in Christ, and all that is in the life He brought to us and placed in us. We sit to have imparted into us divine truths of who He is to us and what He has become in us. Here, we make the necessary investments for spiritual growth. Nothing creates a new-level paradigm in life and ministry like a personal encounter with the living God. Extraordinary encounters with God lead to extraordinary levels in life. It's our personal responsibility to constantly create the most empowering environment to experience the face of God.

7. Fastings

The final characteristic of our prayer culture is the fast. We follow the biblical model of fasting—that of fasting without food. Recently, people are getting so cut up with calling a fast practically anything else under the sun, such as: fasting from TV, social media or playing games etc. All these things are admirable especially when you need to focus on other important things. But we shouldn't call them a fast. The biblical pattern of fasting is fasting without food primarily because of the role food plays in our day to day living. For most, food has become such an idol. Literally, it has become a god that consumes a major part of our time and thoughts. If you think I'm just making this up, try abstaining from it for a few days and see how your entire being reacts. We have way more church meetings with food than we have prayer meetings without it. In fact, prayer gatherings are the least attended gatherings in most developed nations of the world. Most churches, including mega churches barely ever gather together to pray. In my college days in Nigeria, prayer meetings were the largest gatherings. People loved coming out en mass to pray and actually enjoyed praying. Our weekends were mostly given to fasting whole days. And as a result, we experienced a very powerful move of God. Jesus fasted for forty days without food, and so did Moses, as did Elijah. Paul the Apostle and all the other apostles fasted often. Living a life of fasting was their norm — Acts 13:1-4. Exceptional things happen when we fast without food, and press into God in prayer. I'm totally convinced that there are levels in ministry that no one can attain without fasting. I'm equally convinced that fasting combined with prayer equals the highest breakthrough formula in the kingdom of heaven.

END OF BOOK 1

BOOK 2

How to
Hear from God

Flowing in
God's Frequency

Chapter 1

MOSES' MOUNTAIN

"So the Lord spoke to Moses face to
face, as a man speaks to his friend ..."
Exodus 33:11 NKJV.

Moses was a man who was very familiar with hearing from God. In fact, it was his norm. God would either talk with Moses at the tent of meeting or on Mount Sinai as He descended in a pillar of cloud. All of Israel witnessed this unique relationship between God and Moses. God had at one time boasted about His relationship with Moses to both Aaron, his brother, and Miriam, his sister, and bragged about how His relationship with Moses differed from any other.

> And he said, Hear now my words: If
> there be a prophet among you, I the
> Lord will make myself known unto him
> in a vision, and will speak unto him in
> a dream. My servant Moses is not so,
> who is faithful in all mine house. With
> him will I speak mouth to mouth, even
> apparently, and not in dark speeches;

Wouldn't you want to enjoy such a relationship with God—face-to-face fellowship with God? The first man and woman, Adam and Eve, had such a relationship with God. God would show up in a tangible form and visit with them daily. Abraham had a one-on-one conversation with God in human form — Genesis 18:22-23, 33. Why shouldn't we expect that today? Many saints have testified to the fact that they received a personal visit from Jesus in a tangible form. Paul the Apostle did. Jesus showed Himself alive to many in His glorified body right before His second ascension— Acts 1:2-4. Have such manifestations of God ceased? I think not!

And there arose not a prophet
since in Israel like unto Moses,
whom the Lord knew face to face
— Deuteronomy 34:10 KJV.

May a face-to-face encounter with God become your norm. He is as much the God inside you as He is the God beside you. His name is "Yahweh Shammah." It means the Lord is here or present. I see a season of encounters. I see a season of a relentless pressing in, into the presence of God. I see a grabbing of ancient mantles. I see a taking-by-force the powers of the ages to come. It shall be glorious, people!

How Moses heard from God

There's a biblical pattern in Moses' mountain experiences

with God that clearly shows us how God speaks to His own people. I believe that this pattern is still relevant today. The first thing we should address is the myth that it is difficult or impossible to hear God's voice. The fact is that God is always speaking. The most natural thing for any child is to hear the voice of his or her parent. And yes, we too are God's children — John 1:12-13. Jesus said, "My sheep hear my voice" — John 10:3. The issue, however, is that many are failing to live in the frequency where God speaks. Like radio waves, you'll need the right frequency to transmit and receive information. Not too many saints are willing to pay the price for His presence. Did you know that you were born of the Spirit of God into a spirit-world? See John 3:3-8. And that world of the spirit should be your natural habitat. You're actually in the spirit—you live in that realm already — Romans 9:8; Galatians 5:25. However, you're not living in the consciousness of your original abode. Living and walking in the spirit should come as naturally as a baby breathing air and walking in the natural realm.

> And the Lord said unto Moses, Come up to me into the mount, and be there: and I will give thee tables of stone, and a law, and commandments which I have written; that thou mayest teach them. And Moses went up into the mount, and a cloud covered the mount. And the glory of the Lord abode upon mount Sinai, and the cloud covered it six days: and the seventh day he called unto Moses out of the midst of the cloud — Exodus 24:12,15-16 KJV.

Notice the specific instructions God gave to Moses. First, the Lord told him to come up to Him on the mountain. That means that Moses was to go on a journey to encounter God. Every true encounter with God begins with a journey of decisions and actions. You must decide that you want God. David said that the one thing he desired and sought after was to live in God's presence the rest of his days — Psalms 27:4. He desired God's constant and abiding presence and took the necessary steps to make it happen. God called Moses on a journey to Mount Sinai to meet with Him. It was a one-on-one meeting with God. God would often tell him to make sure no one or nothing else was to come with him on that journey. At times, God would instruct Moses to see to it that not even the sheep or goats were grazing at the foot of the mountain. And as Moses climbed that mountain, he lost the awareness of every external noise and completely disengaged from the hustle and bustle of everyday life. This was where I got my love for camp meetings. In these camp meetings, where hundreds of people shut out the world and gather for the sole purpose of meeting with God, I've seen God do in three days what others never get to experience in a lifetime. Secondly, God tells him to "be there." God was telling Moses to show presence. He was to shut out everything else and show up for their meeting— to be still and quiet his heart and mind in God's presence.

> And he was there with the Lord forty days and forty nights; he did neither eat bread, nor drink water. And he wrote upon the tables the words of the covenant, the ten commandments. And it came to pass, when Moses came down from mount Sinai with the two tables of testimony in Moses' hand,

> when he came down from the mount,
> that Moses wist not that the skin of his
> face shone while he talked with him.
> And when Aaron and all the children of
> Israel saw Moses, behold, the skin of
> his face shone; and they were afraid to
> come nigh him—Exodus 34:28-30 KJV.

We as human beings actually have no idea how much internal noise we struggle with on a daily basis, in the flesh. With all the cares of this world coupled with all the pressure it brings, we've got way too much going on in our lives. Scattered thoughts, with all of their inherent anxiety and dread, constantly bombard us at every turn. These noises drown out the voice of God, blocking us from hearing from Him. In order to hear from God, we must show Him that we have walked away, subduing external noises and voices, and be there in both body and soul. In everything we must say, "Lord, here am I, speak to me." Furthermore, when God told Moses to "be-there," He was instructing Moses to meet Him on His own terms. Moses was to wait on God for as long as it would take. How many times have we wanted God to meet us on our own terms, rather than His. We want God to hear us and fix our problems with the wave of a magic wand. He never told Moses how long he'd have to wait. But while Moses was showing up in his personal pursuit of God, he had to wait on God's timing. God wasn't on Moses' clock; Moses was on God's clock. Thirdly, Moses neither ate nor drank anything. In other words, he fasted. And he had the word of God or the law present. He also communed with God in prayer. The elements of going on a journey, being present, waiting on God's timing, fasting, reading God's Word and praying all help to create the most empowering environment to encounter God and hear from

Him. These elements place our spirits and souls in the place of victory. They make our faith robust and vibrant. The connection of our spirits with God's Spirit becomes stronger and the voltage of God's life through us becomes more manifest — 2 Corinthians 4:10-12. Here, we find ourselves living in the spirit and taking progressive steps in the spirit — Galatians 5:25.

CHAPTER 2

PETER'S TRANCE

P eter's story here is both interesting and revealing. It shows us the type of environment in which the Spirit of God moves and speaks. God's Spirit, it seems, doesn't speak in just any environment. The same elements that were present in Moses' day (showing presence, fasting, praying and ministering to God, etc.) seem to be present here too. God wanted to get something extremely important across to Peter, but He needed a specific atmosphere to do precisely that. God wanted the gospel of the Lord Jesus to go to the Gentile world, and Peter would be the first person to take it there. However, He had to get Peter to deal with his own personal biases about the Gentiles, since the law of Moses forbade any interaction between the Jews and Gentiles.

> On the morrow, as they went on their journey, and drew nigh unto the city, Peter went up upon the housetop to pray about the sixth hour: And he became very hungry, and would have eaten: but while they made ready, he fell into a trance, And saw heaven opened, and a certain vessel descending upon him, as it had been a great sheet knit at

the four corners, and let down to the
earth — Acts 10:9-11 KJV.

Peter went up to the rooftop to pray about the sixth hour. That's twelve noon. Somehow, Peter was observing the seventh prayer watch of the day (12noon to <u>3pm</u>). All of a sudden, Peter became very hungry, and would have had lunch, but at the time lunch wasn't ready. While they were yet preparing his meal, he fell into a trance. I admire how the Holy Spirit operated in this situation. What would have happened if Peter had eaten his lunch? Why would God stop him from eating something as simple and as harmless as a lunch in order to get across to him through a trance? Just lunch you say! Yes, it might have cost him dearly. It might have cost him taking the gospel to the Gentile world. God moves and speaks in very specific atmospheres. It's our responsibility to cooperate with God to make that atmosphere happen. Atmospheric environments and temperatures are governed by laws—laws designed by God Himself. If we master the laws, we can initiate a move of God. God is showing in this story that when we fast, God moves. He is showing us that fasting and praying are the elements that bring God into a scene. He orbits within the constellations of fasting and prayer. Fasting turns down the volumes of this world, and prayer connects us to God. This pattern is unmistakable in all of scripture. It seems that Peter went into a forced fast. It was necessary to help him fine-tune his spirit toward God. It helped to open up his spiritual antenna where he contacted God's transmission waves. In other words, he tuned into God's frequency. Food and thoughts of food create an immense amount of noisy distraction in the body. It consumes time. It often gives the body priority over the spirit, drowning out the Spirit of God. The goal is to keep the body light and healthy while feeding the spirit through our fellowship with God. Remember, man doesn't live by bread alone — Matthew 4:4. Our spirits need to thrive on the wings of communion and fellowship. Fellowship is prayer, ministering to God in praise, worship and thanksgiving, living thankfully, fasting, showing presence, reading and studying God's Word, and making confessions of who we are in Christ and what Christ has become to us and in us. If we intentionally live a lifestyle of prayer and fasting, we will constantly experience breakthrough after breakthrough.

☙ CHAPTER 3 ❧

CORNELIUS' VISION

And Cornelius said, Four days ago I was fasting until this hour; and at the ninth hour I prayed in my house, and, behold, a man stood before me in bright clothing, And said, Cornelius, thy prayer is heard, and thine alms are had in remembrance in the sight of God. Send therefore to Joppa, and call hither Simon, whose surname is Peter; he is lodged in the house of one Simon a tanner by the sea side: who, when he cometh, shall speak unto thee. Immediately therefore I sent to thee; and thou hast well done that thou art come. Now therefore are we all here present before God, to hear all things that are commanded thee of God
— Acts 10:30-33 KJV.

H ere again we see the patterns in which God both moves and speaks. What was Cornelius, a Gentile and Roman centurion, doing when a man in bright clothing appeared to him in a vision and told him to go send for Peter the Apostle? Was he vacationing on a beach somewhere?

Was he at a football game somewhere? Was he at a party barbecuing? None of these things are essentially wrong, and God may speak to us while doing all of the above, but the scriptures reveal that very serious kingdom business is conducted when we give ourselves to fasting and prayer. Cornelius was apparently on his fifth day of fasting, and while observing the eighth prayer watch of the day (3pm to 6pm), when the angel of God showed up. Why does God often show up in a fast? Why does He often reveal His plans to the one given over to a life of prayer and fasting? Again, it's because to speak, He must lead us to the still waters. It is the stillness of both soul and body. Here, the troublesome pestilence of this world is quieted. Here, our born-again spirits take precedence. Here, in the Holy of Holies, from among the cherubs, God speaks. According to the biblical pattern revealed, we are guaranteed that when we are given over to a season of fasting and prayer, God speaks. However, we must transition from a season of flowing in God's frequency to actually abiding in God's presence—an active and manifest abiding presence void of the influences of this present world with all of its distractions. Notably, it took a fast to bring about a divine arrangement for the salvation of Cornelius' household. This divine arrangement was orchestrated by God's Spirit on both ends by a fast. Imagine, how many more divine arrangements would be taking place if we made fasting a proper aspect of our diet. I'm absolutely convinced that in order to have greater results in soul winning, corporate fasts need to become a central part of our lifestyle. The Holy Spirit worked on the souls of men, often bringing about the salvation of entire towns and cities on the wing of the church's frequent fasts and prayers. It often amazes me how involved the Holy Spirit was in the life of the apostles and disciples of old—how they all worked under the direct leadership of His influence. It was clearly evident who was in-charge in the church of "Acts." It will become evident again through mighty signs and wonders.

CHAPTER 4

THE
BREAKTHROUGH FORMULA

The highest breakthrough formula in the kingdom of God is prayer and fasting. A more careful study of the scriptures will reveal this. There are higher places in the spirit we may never walk in, or break through, in manifest power, without this formula. Let's see how Jesus said it.

> And he said unto them, This kind can come forth by nothing, but by prayer and fasting — Mark 9:29 KJV.

The phrase, "this kind," speaks of depths or levels that are uncommon or unusual. Think of it as breaking forth into the next phase or the next realm or the next dimension. In life, most people work very hard at breaking through the next ceiling of life. Feeling stuck, stagnant and unproductive is not a part of our innate nature. We all want to make some progress no matter how little or insignificant. Fasting and prayer are divine elements that help to make this next level breakthrough happen. Ultimately, all promotions in kingdom life come from God. However, fasting and prayer are tools designed by God to help us accomplish the unusual kind. There's tremendous power in mixing our prayers with a fast, and the benefits are too numerous to mention. That scripture is pointing to something even far more powerful. In the casting out of this demon mentioned, Jesus categorically pointed out that there's no other way or method of getting the job accomplished except through the combined formula of prayer and fasting. It means that there's no other way than this way. There's no other means or method known to God. Simply put, fasting and prayer is the only way. When every other method fails, this one will not. In other words, it's the highest breakthrough formula, generating all the necessary force needed to move things to the next level. If we fast and pray for the right biblical reasons, we will always witness the corresponding results. Let's be clear: there were things God could not bring to bear without a fast. We will examine some benefits of a fast in the chapters following. I believe that "this kind" is upon us to whom the end of the world has come. "This kind" in life and in ministry happens when we fast and pray.

ᔥCHAPTER 5ᔥ

THE 3 DAY FAST

Then Esther bade them return Mordecai
this answer, Go, gather together all
the Jews that are present in Shushan,
and fast ye for me, and neither eat nor
drink three days, night or day: I also and
my maidens will fast likewise; and so
will I go in unto the king, which is not
according to the law: and if I perish, I
perish — Esther 4:15-16 KJV.

Esther, the queen, called for a three-day fast. And it was
a three-day fast for all the Jews in Mede and Persia.
This was, in a sense, a national fast. And in this particular
fast, every Jew without exception was to fast without food
or water. This kind of a fast is usually referred to as a dry
fast. A dry fast is a fast without an ounce of food or a drop
of any liquids. She wanted all of Israel to fast for her for a
whole three-day period or for seventy-two hours. A devious
plan to completely annihilate the Jews had been put in
place by Haman, the Jews' archenemy. Mordecai, Esther's
guardian, had beseeched Esther to go to the King and plead
the cause of the Jews in the hope that this treacherous plan
by Haman would be averted. At first, she hesitated and then
decided that she was going to take the risk of approaching

the king even if it cost her, her life. It was a well-known rule that no one could dare approach the king unless he summoned them. The penalty of doing so was imminent death. She and her maidens also went on a three-day day fast. This type of a fast gave the queen supernatural favor in the eyes of the king, and resulted in averting the death of all the Jews at Shushan. Haman, the plotter, ended up being hanged on gallows in the market place for all to see. A three-day dry fast is a fast one should undertake when facing an impossible situation or obstacle. It's a fast we should do when we're faced with life-threatening circumstances. This fast must be done with total consecration to God. We should not be employed, engaged or involved in any other activity when we undertake to do this fast. All of our attention and concentration should be solely on God throughout the duration of this fast. This fast brings God on the scene into an impossible situation, and averts it. I would recommend a complete lock-in for such a fast. Here, give yourself to the reading and the study of God's word; to praise and thanksgiving; and to relentless prayer. Watch God turn that impossible situation right before your very eyes. He did it for Israel and for Esther, and He'll do it for you too.

❧ CHAPTER 6 ❧

THE 21 DAY FAST

> In those days I Daniel was mourning three full weeks. I ate no pleasant bread, neither came flesh nor wine in my mouth, neither did I anoint myself at all, till three whole weeks were fulfilled—Daniel 10:2-3 KJV.

The twenty-one day fast is famously attributed to Daniel. Twenty-one days is also three times-seven days. That's a "thrice" perfection. It's perfection multiplied. It's perfection within a perfection within a perfection. I believe that this fast has to do with a complete turnaround for spirit, soul and body. In this fast, Daniel was praying for the restoration of the Jewish nation. Right after he had discovered from the Book of Jeremiah that their seventy-year captivity in exile was almost up, he decided to go into a twenty-one-day fast to find out the exact timing of their release. The archangel, Gabriel, was sent to tell him the exact timing and dates. And in this timing, the angel Gabriel also foreshadowed the coming of the Messiah to take away the sin of the whole world. In this fast, he mourned and repented for his sins and Israel's sins against God. God heard his prayer, and moved mightily on behalf of Israel, releasing them far ahead of the seventy-year captivity previously pre-determined for them.

This fast is necessary when your soul is at a crossroads. If your heart is full of doubts, and uncertainties; if your heart is troubled or you're aware that something is deeply amiss; if you feel like you've been trying to make things happen by self-effort and that in spite of your best efforts, you're running on empty, or you can't seem to fully pinpoint the root cause, the twenty-one day fast would be the perfect fast for you. This twenty-one day fast does not necessarily require going without food or liquids, although, some do. The goal of abstaining from enjoyable meals and wines is to fully give yourself to prayer, and to avoid all necessary distractions. It's to help keep the priority of the task in front of you. Daniel fasted in search of a truth upon which the destiny of the Jewish nation rested. He wanted to know God's heart concerning the situation. And the knowledge of that truth made him free. Maybe, you too feel like you're at a crossroads. Weighty matters of the heart perplex you. Life decisions stare you in the face, and you don't know where to turn. You feel mentally troubled. Maybe, you're in a deep hole of depression. This fast will shed light on the root-causes, and offer you a clear path out of the situation. This fast requires that you eat lightly if you must and make the focus about God. When it comes to fasting, it's all about devoting all of you to all of God as you seek the answers for a turnaround. You may be engaged in other activities or responsibilities, but your focus on God should trump it all.

CHAPTER 7

THE 40-DAY FAST

The forty-day fast is a fast specially situated for someone who wants so much more of God. It's for someone who wants to witness apostolic grace and power. It's for someone who wants to see the earth covered in the glory of God as the waters cover the sea. When the church becomes lukewarm and starts explaining away the days of the supernatural acts of God, this fast is needed. When we substitute the wisdom and the works of men for that of the Holy Spirit, we need a forty-day fast. When philosophy and the traditions of men thrive instead of a living faith in God, this fast is needed. When the church loses the signs that accompany the resurrection life of Jesus Christ, this fast should be called for. When demonic doctrines and vices run rampant without restraint, this fast should urgently be employed. When the church in its contemporary culture is more concerned about how people feel far more than how God feels, someone needs to go on a forty-day fast. Usually, a forty-day fast is initiated by the Holy Spirit. He's the one prompting a person or group of persons to go on a forty day fast. All three biblical prophets: Jesus, Elijah and Moses were divinely instructed to go on a forty-day fast. Moses actually went on an eighty-day fast (forty days back to back). His natural life was fully sustained by God's divine life during the eighty-day fast. Moses' fast literally transformed him from the inside out. He wanted to see God's face. And his unrelenting hunger to know God resulted in his total transformation. He came down that mountain aglow with the glory of God.

> And Jesus being full of the Holy Ghost returned from Jordan, and was led by the Spirit into the wilderness, Being forty days tempted of the devil. And in those days he did eat nothing: and when they were ended, he afterward hungered. And Jesus returned in the power of the Spirit into Galilee: and there went out a fame of him through all the region round about. Luke 4:1-2,14 KJV.

Jesus was full of the Holy Spirit prior to going on a forty-day fast. And this is where most of us are missing it. Many think that because they're baptized in the Holy Spirit with the evidence of speaking with other tongues, that they've got it made. Jesus, was both filled and full of the Spirit. This refilling of the Spirit happens as we maintain an active fellowship with God. Now notice Jesus came back into town in the power of the Spirit. And suddenly His fame went abroad. Fasting converts the refillings of the Spirit into the power of the Spirit. These are two different dimensions of the Spirit of God. Jesus had both — Acts 10:38. There's a momentum in the spirit that comes through fasting that can't be explained by science or any other natural phenomenon. This type of a fast invites the wind of God to blow behind your sails. It produces exploits that transcend human comprehension. It advances God's kingdom in such a forceful manner that it scares the daylights out of the devil. It's power that subdues all the works

64

of darkness — Psalm 66:3. It's power that puts all the miracles, signs and wonders of Jesus on full display. It's His power that advances the cause of the gospel at the speed of spirit — 2 Thessalonians 3:1. It's His power that brings whole communities into the knowledge of His saving grace. If you want to walk in the miraculous power of God, and do mighty exploits for the kingdom, frequently observe this fast. Keep your body light and focus on practicing God's presence.

BOOK 3

THE SEVEN LAWS OF ASKING & RECEIVING

HOW TO PRAY & RECEIVE ANSWERS

CHAPTER 1

THE LAW OF SIMPLICITY

Ask, and it shall be given you; seek, and ye shall find; knock, and it shall be opened unto you: For every one that asketh receiveth; and he that seeketh findeth; and to him that knocketh it shall be opened. Or what man is there of you, whom if his son ask bread, will he give him a stone? Or if he ask a fish, will he give him a serpent? If ye then, being evil, know how to give good gifts unto your children, how much more shall your Father which is in heaven give good things to them that ask him? Therefore all things whatsoever ye would that men should do to you, do ye even so to them: for this is the law and the prophets — Matthew 7:7-12 KJV.

This law of simplicity is important, and many believers miss it, because the principle of asking and receiving is so exquisitely simple. In other words, they miss the "asking and receiving prayer design"—that is, how this particular type of prayer works. They assume that prayer, especially the prayer of asking and receiving, is complex.

Truth be told, many just haven't yet figured out how to receive from God or rather, how it works to receive by faith. And the lack of knowledge in this area has rendered so many prayers void of answers. In the prayer of asking and receiving, we must believe with the heart, that we receive, and begin to act as if it's so — Mark 11:24. And we keep our faith both alive and active through our confession of faith and thanksgiving. Here, thinking faith, talking faith and acting faith must remain consistent until the answer manifests in the natural realm.

When Jesus introduces the subject on "how-to-pray" to His disciples, He opens with the following words: "Our Father, who art in heaven" — Matthew 6:9. This opening introduction on prayer reveals that all true prayer begins with a revelation of a Father-son or Father-daughter relationship. In other words, prayer is based on relationship. And although, every believer has a right-standing with God as far as his or her judicial position is concerned, it is the experiential relationship that builds the confidence for answered prayer.

A life of constant communion with God strengthens your personal relationship with God just like it does when you're spending quality times with a friend or a parent. That constant fellowship with a friend opens up the deeper sides of him or her that otherwise would never be revealed. You get to know their strengths and weaknesses, and their true authentic self, including their core nature and deepest desires. As we spend time with God, we get to know Him more intimately as a real person—as one would a best friend. The end goal of prayer is getting to know God as a person and growing in your personal knowledge of Him. An active, strong, vibrant and robust relationship with God is the key to answered prayer. It literally inspires your level of confidence for answered prayer.

70

In a true two-sided communion, God begins to reveal the many different sides of Himself to you—sides you never thought possible. The stronger the experiential fellowship with God, the stronger becomes the relational bond. The deeper the fellowship, the deeper your knowledge of God grows. Did you know that the greatest revelation, Moses, the man of God, ever had of God was God's back parts? That back part of God was a veil or posed as a veil, blinding him from seeing the fullness of God's glory — 2 Corinthians 3:7-18. However, in the New Testament, God has been revealed to us in the person of Jesus Christ. Moses saw God's back parts, but in Christ, we see God's face in the person of Jesus Christ. That is, we see Him as He truly is. These various sides of God give us a better understanding of His nature, His character, His person and His power. Spending time in prayer reveals God's capacity. It reveals His immense ability to do the impossible. It shows us what God can do and what God *will* do, because of His great love for us. And, we know this because we know Him. It is this intimate personal knowledge of God that drives our prayer life into high gear.

Our faith in Him is based on our knowledge of Him. We believe in His ability to do amazing things because we've grown to know His immeasurable power and endless love. This knowledge we've possessed overtime breeds immense confidence in our asking and in our receiving from God. Elijah had such confidence. Jesus had an unshakable confidence in the Father's ability to answer prayer and, Jesus knew His Father's ability infinitely. His knowledge of the Father's backing gave Him confidence even in the face of death itself. And Jesus walked in the full consciousness of His Father's ability in everything He did, and everywhere He went. Effective prayer—prayer that works is effective based on the strength of your relationship with God. And our relationship with God grows through our fellowship with Him. Relationship has to do with our judicial position while fellowship has to do with our experiential position. Think about it this way: if a child has to continue to live in this world, it would be necessary that the child continues to take in oxygen. He or she cannot say, "I'm tired of breathing in oxygen today. I think I am going to stop breathing now." That would result in premature death, literally. This is why you'll hear us often say, "Prayer is our oxygen." We never take breaks or vacations from fellowshipping with God. Our very lives depend on it. To know God intimately, we must grow in our communion with Him. Enoch did this for 300 years — Genesis 5:22-24. He had an unbroken, habitual fellowship with God. You will know Him, when you spend time with Him. And the more you grow in your knowledge of Him, the more your confidence in Him will grow also. It is this confidence that makes it work when you ask for things in prayer.

Therefore, the first law of asking and receiving starts with the simplicity of asking. The command given is to ask. Just ask. Ask for what you want like a child would asking a father or mother. It's that simple.

THE SIMPLICITY OF ASKING

Let's take a good look at how King Solomon applied this law of simplicity in regard to asking and receiving in prayer. God had offered him a blank cheque to ask whatever he wanted after he offered a thousand burnt offerings to God in a single day.

> King Solomon went to Gibeon to offer
> a sacrifice because that was the most

> important high place. He offered a
> thousand burnt offerings on that altar.
> While Solomon was at Gibeon, the Lord
> came to him at night in a dream. God
> said, "Solomon, ask me what you want
> me to give you" — 1 Kings 3:4-5 ERV.

Here, God told Solomon to ask. Asking is simply stating clearly exactly what you want, with no confusion or ambiguities. State it boldly, clearly and confidently. That's all.

Can we find these things in King Solomon's request? I think we can. See what Solomon asked for and how he asked for it.

> Here's what I want: Give me a God-
> listening heart so I can lead your
> people well, discerning the difference
> between good and evil. For who on
> their own is capable of leading your
> glorious people? — 1 Kings 3:9 MSG.

How specific can one get, right? Could he have made it any more plain or simple? Its simplicity was defined by its specificity. Solomon clarified his win, and confidently asked for it. It's important that we put some thought into the requests we often make. Process it until it becomes refined and clear—short and sweet. Think through it until you know exactly what it is you really want. In essence, own what you want. It's clear; it's specific, and you're so certain of it that no one can talk you out of it. If you're not sure of it, it won't work. A double-minded man is unstable in all his ways and never receives anything from the Lord — James 1:6-8.

"Ask, and it shall be given you" —
Matthew 7:7 KJV.

Think about this for a moment: God says if you ask, you shall receive. There are no ifs, buts or maybes. Imagine approaching every prayer you prayed with such confidence. You ask, believing you receive — Matthew 21:22. God guarantees the answer by placing His integrity on the line. May this truth shape how we approach prayer. Why even ask if you're not asking to receive? Did you know that it's an insult to fail to believe God? He that comes to God must believe that He is — Hebrews 11:6. Why pray for the sick one and not believe for healing? The one backing that promise is God. The one behind the promise cannot lie. He has both the capacity and ability to answer prayer. God watches over His word to perform it — Jeremiah 1:12.

"For every one that asketh receiveth" —
Matthew 7:8 KJV.

God's daring you to ask Him. Everyone who asks, receives. This is the law of faith at its best—ask, believing you receive. Scriptures show that it's in the character of God to answer prayer at the instant the prayer of faith is offered. If Daniel had known that, he wouldn't have continued praying — Daniel 10:12. The key to answered prayer is in our knowing that God has heard us when we pray — 1 John 5:14-15. Simply take Him at His word. When King Solomon asked for wisdom, God generously gave it to him. When Hannah asked for a baby boy, God generously gave her a baby boy, and five more children after that. Jesus lived constantly under an open heaven. He boldly proclaimed that the Father heard Him at all times. All of His miracles, and there were many of them, were all a result of answered prayer. His standing confidently at the grave of Lazarus after he'd been dead four days, stemmed from His confidence in His Father's willingness and ability to answer prayer. Developing this kind of prayer consciousness is important. God is eager, willing, ready and able to answer prayer. He gave us all a blank cheque to write on it exactly what we want. He extended to us the legal right to ask, and the legal right to receive the answers to our prayers. He literally opened up a free invitation to you to ask, and guaranteed that if you'd asked without doubting, you'd receive the answer to your prayer. Are you ready to pray and receive swift answers? Well, pause in your soul and acknowledge Him now as your ever-present helper in the room. Go ahead and ask, believing you receive.

❦ CHAPTER 2 ❧

THE LAW OF SPECIFICITY

"Ask, and it shall be given you; seek, and ye shall find; knock, and it shall be opened unto you: For every one that asketh receiveth; and he that seeketh findeth; and to him that knocketh it shall be opened. Or what man is there of you, whom if his son ask bread, will he give him a stone? Or if he ask a fish, will he give him a serpent? If ye then, being evil, know how to give good gifts unto your children, how much more shall your Father which is in heaven give good things to them that ask him? Therefore all things whatsoever ye would that men should do to you, do ye even so to them: for this is the law and the prophets" — Matthew 7:7-12 KJV.

In asking and receiving, the law of specificity applies. It's the law of asking for things in a specific way. Or simply put, it's asking for specific things in a specific way. Notice the use of the language in which Jesus describes the law of specificity: **"Or what man is there of you, whom if his son ask bread, will he give him a stone? Or if he ask a**

fish, will he give him a serpent?" The request is specific: "If his son ask for bread or ask for a fish." Regarding the law of asking and receiving, generic prayers don't work.

There's this story in the Bible of a blind man seeking to receive his sight from Jesus. You would think that his desire would be obvious, considering his blindness, yet Jesus demanded that he be specific when He asked, "What would you have me to do for you?"

> Jesus said to him, "What do you want me to do for you?" The man replied, "My Master, please, let me see again!" Jesus responded, "Your faith heals you. Go in peace, with your sight restored." All at once, the man's eyes opened and he could see again, and he began at once to follow Jesus, walking down the road with him — Mark 10:51-52 TPT.

Isn't it ironic how often we assume that because God knows all about what we're going through, we believe that He should also know exactly what we need. The fact that He knows doesn't exempt us from making our requests known to Him. It's our responsibility to ask specifically for things we expect to receive. It requires us to ask for one thing at a time and do it in a specific way.

> Be careful for nothing; but in every thing by prayer and supplication with thanksgiving let your requests be made known unto God — Philippians 4:6 KJV.

It is of primary importance that you make your requests known to God in a very specific way. That way, you'll have no doubt that God did indeed answer that prayer specifically. The more detailed the request, the better.

In the Gospel of Luke, he adds an additional component to the one in the Gospel of Matthew:

> And I say unto you, Ask, and it shall be given you; seek, and ye shall find; knock, and it shall be opened unto you. For every one that asketh receiveth; and he that seeketh findeth; and to him that knocketh it shall be opened. If a son shall ask bread of any of you that is a father, will he give him a stone? or if he ask a fish, will he for a fish give him a serpent? Or if he shall ask an egg, will he offer him a scorpion?
> — Luke 11:9-12 KJV.

Take a minute and see what we have the right to ask for as sons and daughters of Jesus. A quick look reveals a great breakfast when He speaks of bread instead of a stone; fish instead of a serpent, and an egg instead of a scorpion. Bread, fish and eggs. It can't get any more delectable than that. Then He adds that if we humans born with a sinful nature know how to give good things to our own children, how much more shall our heavenly Father give good things to those who ask Him. We serve a "how-much-more" kind of a Father who wants to do exceedingly, abundantly above all we can ask or think — Ephesians 3:20. Again, it is the sequence of asking for one thing at a time, and asking for it in a specific way. This would infer that you take out time to think about want you actually want before you begin to pray. It would imply that you carefully and methodically process exactly want you want. In other words, be very clear about your request. No rushed or thoughtless request here. Put some thought into it.

Unfortunately, some people muddle their requests, and what they're asking for isn't clear. Any chair won't do. You'll have to be a little more specific. Any car won't do, you'll have to be more specific. Any house won't do, you'll have to be more specific. Any amount of money won't work, you'll have to be more specific. That's how to ask and receive from God. Think about how an entire city or community is planned before it's constructed. Imagine what kind of a city one would build without a clear and specific plan? A muddled plan breeds confusion and makes it both unachievable and unattainable. Again, imagine a flight with no flight plan. To have your prayers answered, you're going to have to ask for specific things in a specific way. What you ask for in prayer must be both clear and specific.

Have you ever found yourself in a given situation where you thought you wanted something so bad— something you just had to have? You were so sure of it at the time that anyone who dared to try convincing you otherwise received an unpleasant reaction from you. Then after only a few days, you found yourself losing all interest. Or how about after getting something you thought you couldn't live without, and later regretted that decision. I think that on some level we've all had such experiences. And this is the reason why in applying this law of specificity, time becomes a crucial element—like the growing of a seed out of the soil or like the growing of a baby within the womb of its mother. The goal of asking for what you want is to be so certain of it that no one and no circumstance can talk you out of it. It has to be conceived in the womb of your spirit, and then grow until it dominates every single fiber of your being. It literally permeates your thoughts. You'll have to see your-self possessing this "want" by faith as though you already have it. The witness of God's Spirit with your spirit must be unshakable and unchangeable. The request becomes a passionate and confident request that's unwavering. When you become this specific in your request, you'll always have the answer to your prayer. Whatsoever you desire, when you pray, remember? — Mark 11:24 KJV. A strong desire for something after much contemplation should drive the making of your requests in prayer.

❧CHAPTER 3❧

THE LAW OF RECIPROCITY

"Ask, and it shall be given you; seek,
and ye shall find; knock, and it shall be
opened unto you: For every one that
asketh receiveth; and he that seeketh
findeth; and to him that knocketh it
shall be opened. Or what man is there
of you, whom if his son ask bread, will
he give him a stone? Or if he ask a fish,
will he give him a serpent? If ye then,
being evil, know how to give good gifts
unto your children, how much more
shall your Father which is in heaven
give good things to them that ask him?
Therefore all things whatsoever ye
would that men should do to you, do ye
even so to them: for this is the law and
the prophets" — Matthew 7:7-12 KJV.

The third law of asking and receiving is the law of reciprocity, and it's one that requires a faith response. It requires a tangible action from the one making the request. It demands a corresponding action from the one making the request. This is how Jesus states it: **"Therefore all things whatsoever ye would that men should do to you, do ye**

**even so to them: for this is the law and the prophets"
— Matthew 7:12 KJV.** What this means is that whatever
you want to see happen in your life, you're going to first
have to make it happen for someone else. The key word
here is "first." In other words, you're going to have to
first give toward your expected harvest. For instance, if
you're praying for a new pair of shoes, give the best pair
of shoes you currently have away to someone else. If you
need a new car, give away the one you have to someone
else. Depending on the condition of the car, you may have
to fix it up a bit. Make it look great and drivable the best
way you can, and sow it as a seed into someone else's
life. The seed must first be planted. It must get into the
ground. Get the seed into the ground to yield a harvest of
miracles. Don't go giving something you won't use or that
doesn't work to someone else because God is not going
to honor it. It must be something that is of some value to
you. You'll notice that God often opens up the womb of a
barren woman when she legally adopts someone's child.
I have seen this work repeatedly. This is the law of reciprocity in action. It is one of the fastest and surest ways to
have your prayers answered. Remember, every seed repro-
duces after its kind — Genesis 1:24-25. Therefore, sow
toward others what you intend to harvest from God. Don't
go sowing apples expecting oranges—that would be a vio-
lation of the law of the "exact kind." Not only do you first
seed toward your expected harvest, you'll have to seed into
the life of someone else, the exact thing you're expecting
to receive from God. If you're expecting a specific amount
of money, start tithing and sowing that percentage level. In
other words, tithe upward. Start giving on the amount you'd
like to receive. If I make an income of hundred thousand
dollars a year, my tithe would be ten thousand dollars off
of that. So, if I would like to double that income, I'll have

to start tithing the exact corresponding amount. In this case, that would be twenty thousand dollars a year. If we would apply that law of reciprocity, we would always have the answers to our prayer.

In college, the Holy Spirit once impressed me to give my most cherished traditional clothes to a brother who could never afford to pay me back. Although I gave it with great joy, it pained me to do it. I had worn that piece of clothing with a great deal of pride because it made me important and significant. It was the only material thing I owned that was valuable at the time. Upon fully relinquishing it, I felt a joy that surpassed the pain of giving it. At the time, I had no idea that God wasn't taking anything away from me, but that He was wanting to get something far better for me. I had to obey God in order to create the capacity to receive. I had to make room to receive something far more valuable than I had by relinquishing something I thought was the best I could have. You receive the best by giving your best, not by giving your worst. That same week, my uncle from the U.S. got me a brand-new suit that became my most cherished outfit for many years afterward. No one in town had one like it or even came close to it—in it I felt like a brand-new man. Reciprocity always works. The entire law and the prophets hang on it. This means that if this law of reciprocity doesn't work for you then, the whole of scripture is at stake of being undermined. Whatever you make happen for someone else, God will make it happen for you. The law of reciprocity commits God to act in your favor.

ᚥCHAPTER 4᚛

THE LAW OF FAITH

But let him ask in faith, nothing wavering.
For he that wavereth is like a wave of
the sea driven with the wind and tossed.
For let not that man think that he shall
receive any thing of the Lord. A double
minded man is unstable in all his ways
— James 1:6-8 KJV.

R emember, I mentioned that once you know how to ask
for things in prayer, you'll always receive answers
from God. And one of the ways to ask for things from God
is ask in faith. When asking anything from God, you must
ask in faith, refusing to waver no matter how contrary the
evidence. Asking in faith is believing that you have what
you've asked for. That is, that you possess what you've
asked for as a current reality. It is thinking, talking and
acting like you've already received it. It's believing that
you receive. It has nothing to do with physically seeing it
or emotionally feeling it. It's solely based upon the integrity of the Word of God. It's so because God said so, period.
Faith is anchored on what God said. And this is the reason
why you must hold on to the confession of your faith. Ask,
believing you've received the answer. Then think, talk and
act as if it is so because it *is* so. Your thoughts, speech

and actions must all agree until you experience the fruit of your requests. Faith sees. Faith is the evidence of things spiritually seen — Hebrews 11:1. You can see what the Word promised and lay hold of it by faith; then, continue to hold onto the confession of your faith without wavering.

Now, let's consider why asking in faith is so important and how it works. We all know that faith pleases God, and faith is not faith if it is not now — Hebrews 11:1. Believing that whosoever comes to God must believe that He is — right now in the present, not just that He was in the past, or that He will be in the future. This is the basis for a living, working faith.

> Therefore I say unto you, What things soever ye desire, when ye pray, believe that ye receive them, and ye shall have them — Mark 11:24 KJV.

The above scripture is telling us that when we pray our desires, we should pray believing in that moment that we receive. In other words, we receive the answer to our prayers at the instant the prayer is offered. Only after we've prayed, believing that we've received what we asked for in prayer will we actually have our petitions materialize. God wants us to believe we receive *before* we see the physical manifestation of our requests. Faith is the evidence of things not seen — Hebrews 11:1. So, faith deals with the invisible realm and with invisible reality or rather, spiritual reality. Faith is the evidence of things spiritually seen, not physically seen. Faith functions completely outside the five senses. This is why when we pray, God, in response to our faith delivers the answer to us in a spirit-substance form. We must lay hold of this spirit-substance by faith, and never waver. We thank Him for receiving what has been

85

already bequeathed to us until the invisible answers to our prayer become visible. And we proactively wait for the physical manifestation of what we've prayed and believed for with thanksgiving and with the unwavering confession of our faith.

> While we look not at the things which are seen, but at the things which are not seen: for the things which are seen are temporal; but the things which are not seen are eternal — 2 Corinthians 4:18 KJV.

God is essentially a spirit composed of spiritual substance, and all that He bequeathed to us through the death, burial and resurrection of the Lord Jesus Christ is first delivered to us in spirit-substance. With God, there are three levels of creation: first, spiritual; secondly, mental; and thirdly, physical. A diligent student of the scriptures will realize that Genesis one is a spiritual creation whereas Genesis two is a physical creation. We see creation in a spirit-substance form (Hebrews 11:3), and then eventually converted to a physical substance form. Please note that the highest form of reality is spiritual reality and the lowest form is physical reality. In prayer, we lay hold of the highest reality—a spirit substance materiality until that reality transforms our thought life and opens the way for God to transport things from the invisible realm into the visible realm. You'll notice that Jesus already thanked God for raising Lazarus back to life long before Lazarus was called out of the region of the dead.

> Then they took away the stone from the place where the dead was laid. And

Jesus lifted up his eyes, and said, Father,
I thank thee that thou hast heard me —
John 11:41 KJV.

The raising up of Lazarus from the dead had already happened in the spirit realm. Jesus already had the answer to His prayer before that resurrection happened physically. He also had the answer to His own resurrection long before He died on the cross and physically rose from the dead. He told His disciples numerous times that He would rise from the dead on the third day. David the shepherd boy saw Goliath fall and his head chopped off with a sword long before it ever happened in the natural. The ten lepers were healed long before they went to show themselves to the priest for confirmation. This is the law of faith. This is the way faith works—completely outside the realm of the body's five senses. Faith is based on the Word of God. Faith is anchored on what God said, and not on feelings or what we see with our eyes. Those who choose to measure their wellbeing by how they feel at least at first, have more faith in their feelings than they have in the Word of God. No life that's ruled by feelings—by the destitution of emotions— can thrive or succeed. If I placed a hundred-dollar-bill in my daughter's school bag and asked her if she believed that I did so, without a doubt, she would say yes. If we believe the word of a man or the word of a medical doctor, how dare we ask for proof when the God, who possesses all of heaven and earth, speaks! God says, "You're healed." Why isn't His word enough? Is He a man that He should lie? By seeking for answers based on how we feel or by what we see, we reduce God to the level of a mere carnal man. Faith says it's so because God said so.

> And this is the confidence that we
> have in him, that, if we ask any thing
> according to his will, he heareth us: And
> if we know that he hear us, whatsoever
> we ask, we know that we have the peti-
> tions that we desired of him — 1 John
> 5:14-15 KJV.

When do we know that we have (already possess in the now) the petitions that we desired of God? Is it when we see it physically manifested? Is it when we tangibly possess it? According to the scripture above, we have it when we know He heard our prayer. And our confidence is in the one who always backs up His word to perform it. Our confidence is in the one whose word has never failed and cannot fail. We ask, because He said if we do, we would receive the answers to our requests. So ask, and you shall receive.

Daniel didn't know that God heard him at the instant prayer was offered. It took him twenty-one days to discover that God heard him on the first day.

> Then said he unto me, Fear not, Daniel:
> for from the first day that thou didst
> set thine heart to understand, and to
> chasten thyself before thy God, thy
> words were heard, and I am come for
> thy words — Daniel 10:12 KJV.

With God, hearing you is the same thing as answering you. We receive in spirit-substance the moment we ask. Sometimes, the manifestation can be instantaneous. But it always happens spiritually first. We know we receive because God said we would. There's no evidence greater or superior to God's Word. All that is in Christ is a complete work—a finished work waiting on you to receive it by faith. Faith takes it now as a present reality and thinks, speaks, acts and rejoices as though it is done because it is. Faith works best when it deals with the finished work of Christ. God wants us to start from the end and work forward. God has already healed you — 1 Peter 2:24; He has delivered you — Colossians 1:13; He has made you rich — 2 Corinthians 8:9; You're already redeemed from the curse — Galatians 3:13. So, if this is true, why then, is it not a reality in many lives? Hebrews 4:2 holds the answer: "They don't mix the Word heard, with Faith." Faith is not believing for something new but knowing and acting on what you've believed for like it's already so, because Jesus has already accomplished it on our behalf; it's a finished work. Ex. If you already had a billion dollars right now, how would you act or think? Well, it's knowing that you're already wealthy, and allowing that truth to condition your thinking, which would naturally force you to make decisions and take actions resulting in wealth creation. There's a big difference in asking God to make you wealthy, (which is wrong, because you're asking God to do what He's already done), and acting because you know you're already wealthy. When did Abraham become the Father of Nations? When he had Isaac or before he had Isaac and (did you notice that nothing happened until God conditioned his mindset by what he had heard and even changed his name). When did David become King? The day he was anointed king (although he was still a shepherd boy in the backside of the desert?) or when he sat on the throne as king? Many are asking God to do what He's already done. How many people do you know who ask God to heal them, to deliver them and to bless them? God in Christ already did it. Do you know it? If you do, then live in thanksgiving until it physically materializes.

Hold fast to the confession of your faith which has a great recompense of reward — Hebrews 10:35.

> Let us hold fast the profession of our faith without wavering; (for he is faithful that promised;) Cast not away therefore your confidence, which hath great recompence of reward — Hebrews 10:23, 35 KJV.

The word "profession" should read confession. God is telling us to hold fast to the confession of our faith (Homologia) without wavering. And homologia means to say the same things as God. Whatever God said about you, and said is yours, you say the exact same thing over your life, your health, your finances and your destiny. You never let up thinking, talking and acting it out as a present reality. The law of faith is synonymous with the law of confidence, certainty and audacity. You ask with an unshaken and an immovable faith. The confession of faith flows from a life full of the word of God and full of God's presence. So, how does asking in faith work? Take some time to build your faith on the subject matter. Faith comes by hearing and by hearing the Word of God — Romans 10:17. Find out what the Word says about what you're believing God for. Faith works best where the will of God is known. And knowing that God wants you to have what you're asking for breeds confidence and dissolves doubts. Then, spend some more time meditating on it — 1 Timothy 4:15. Build that image in your mind until it dominates every fiber of your being. Let His Word dwell in you richly, and out of the abundance of the heart the mouth will speak. Speak the rhema word of God until you're filled with the Holy Spirit again and again. It's such a wonderful thing to be constantly under the influence of the Spirit. When you're this full, your cup starts running over. Fellowship with and in God's Word is a sweet thing. It makes your faith robust and alive. We need to put our faith on steroids.

CHAPTER 5

THE LAW OF THE NAME OF JESUS

For I will do whatever you ask me to do when you ask me in my name. And that is how the Son will show what the Father is really like and bring glory to him. Ask me anything in my name, and I will do it for you!" John 14:13-14 TPT.

J esus made us a guarantee that if we ask Him anything in His name, He'll do what we asked for in prayer. If only we would ask for things in His name with such unwavering confidence. We see a simple truth to having our prayers answered. *And that is to pray, believing you receive.* At the instant of praying the prayer of faith, pray, believing you receive. Pray, believing you have it. Jesus said that if we ask for anything in His name, He'll do it. We need to live in the consciousness of this blessed assurance. In other words, there's no margin for error—no room for "ifs or· maybes." It's a certainty—a sure thing. It's a done deal and it's already settled in heaven. Praying with that attitude will always result in answered prayer. God taught my friends and me to pray that way. We were teenagers then, but that's how we would always pray. The villagers knew it too. They knew that if you could get those little teens to pray for you, it was as good as done. We knew without a single doubt that our prayers would assuredly be answered. Never once did we doubt it. We didn't give a thought to deliberating over the fact. After prayer, we would never stop to even consider whether or not it was answered. We simply moved on to the next subject. And why did we behave that way? Because we knew that at the instant we asked in His name, it was done. There was no need to look for proofs. We didn't need it—we knew it. We had developed that attitude of prayer by approaching God in faith. We had the answer even before we uttered the first word.

> Then they took away the stone from the place where the dead was laid. And Jesus lifted up his eyes, and said, Father, I thank thee that thou hast heard me —
> John 11:41 KJV.

We must take on this unwavering confidence in prayer: "Father, I thank thee that thou hast heard me." Jesus had this confidence even while Lazarus laid dead for four days in the tomb. He knew that the moment He offered the request the Father would answer Him. Basically, it was as good as done. God wants us to know that we must pray believing. It's the believing part that's essential — Matthew 21:22. If someone were to deliver to you a certified check, wouldn't you believe that it was as good as you having the money in your hand? All prayers prayed in faith are like certified checks. You wouldn't question it. You would know it was as good as cash.

We see this attitude again in the cursing of the fig tree. Let's examine the scripture on this.

> And on the morrow, when they were come from Bethany, he was hungry: And seeing a fig tree afar off having leaves, he came, if haply he might find any thing thereon: and when he came to it, he found nothing but leaves; for the time of figs was not yet. And Jesus answered and said unto it, No man eat fruit of thee hereafter for ever. And his disciples heard it —Mark 11:12-14 KJV.

Jesus had come upon a fig tree full of leaves with no fruit—not a single fruit. He cursed it by saying the following words: "May no man eat from you forever!" The Bible tells us that His disciples heard Him say those words, but apparently, they were not impressed. They weren't impressed because they didn't see a shred of evidence that the words spoken by Jesus had worked instantly. That fig tree looked exactly the very same way after Jesus spoke those words over it. However, Jesus knew that that fig tree had died at the instant He cursed it. He didn't require any physical evidence. No physical proof was necessary. He possessed a knowledge far superior than the five senses of the body. He had a sixth-sense — "the faith-sense" — 1 Corinthians 2:12. He knew that His words could not return void of power to fulfill His commands, and that nothing in the natural realm was stronger that the words He spoke in faith.

It was on the following day that Peter got the shock of his life. Completely astonished, he called to Jesus telling him that the fig tree had dried up from the roots and died.

> And in the morning, as they passed by, they saw the fig tree dried up from the roots. And Peter calling to

remembrance saith unto him, Master, behold, the fig tree which thou cursed is withered away. And Jesus answering saith unto them, Have faith in God. For verily I say unto you, That whosoever shall say unto this mountain, Be thou removed, and be thou cast into the sea; and shall not doubt in his heart, but shall believe that those things which he saith shall come to pass; he shall have what-soever he saith — Mark 11:20-23 KJV.

I am of the conviction that Jesus never looked back to see for Himself that the fig tree dried up and died. It wasn't necessary. He knew it had no choice but to die, and that it did die the moment He cursed it. This is the kind of faith we ought to have when we ask for anything in prayer. It's exactly the faith attitude we must take. The moment we pray, it's as good as done—period! This is how Mark 11:24 works. When you pray, believe you receive and you shall have it. The evidence is based on nothing but the Word of God. It is anchored solely on the integrity of God Himself. It's so because God said it's so. And, until we see that God's Word is the only proof we need, we may never see the corresponding manifestation of that word. Why believe the fruit without its root? And which one is far more important? "It's not you that sustains the root, but it's the root that sustains you" — Romans 11:18 CEB. Faith won't work if you anchor it on the fruit rather than on the root. God's Word is the root to the fruit. Jesus responded by saying to Peter, "Have the God-kind of faith" (the literal Greek translation). The highest expression of our faith lies in our spoken word. If you had faith, Jesus declared, you would "say" to this mountain.

> Jesus was matter-of-fact: "Embrace this
> God-life. Really embrace it, and nothing
> will be too much for you. This moun-
> tain, for instance: Just say, 'Go jump in
> the lake'—no shuffling or shilly-shal-
> lying—and it's as good as done — Mark
> 11:22-23 MSG.

The God kind of faith completely transforms your language. It transforms it into the God-language. Something
mysterious happens to your tongue and your language
when you place it into the realm where miracles, signs and
wonders become the natural order of the day. If we intelli-
gently cultivated our faith with great intentionality, every
single word would produce instant miracles. The power
is in the quality of the faith driving your words. Are your
words faith-filled? Words on the wings of faith become the
master key to all miracles.

> "For I will do whatever you ask me to
> do when you ask me in my name. And
> that is how the Son will show what the
> Father is really like and bring glory to
> him. Ask me anything in my name, and
> I will do it for you!" John 14:13-14 TPT.

Furthermore, He said that answering prayers is a huge
part of God's core character. God takes great delight in
answering the prayers of His people. Literally, answering
prayers is how God receives glory from His Son. That's
great news! God receives glory by answering prayers. The
ability to meet the needs of humanity brings so much joy to
the Father and is a part of the way He distinguishes Himself
from all the gods in the world. Asking in His name is the

key. And to do that, you're going to have to have a revelation of that name. Another way of saying this is why ask in Jesus' name? And the answer is simple; once you know what's behind the name it's a no-brainer.

All things in all of creation are subject to
the authority in that name

There's not a single thing in the entire universe that is not subject to the name of Jesus. All the powers of hell combined with all the forces of darkness cannot withstand the power in the name of Jesus. No sickness, terminal or otherwise, can survive the healing power in the name of Jesus. Every single form of bondage, yoke or chain will break in the name of Jesus. That name heals all diseases, breaks all yokes and lifts all burdens. The name is also divinely creative. All of creation was made in His name. In that name, new limbs can grow, and new organs can be recreated.

> While he yet spake, behold, a bright cloud overshadowed them: and behold a voice out of the cloud, which said, This is my beloved Son, in whom I am well pleased; hear ye him
> — Matthew 17:5 KJV.

When the Father's voice came from heaven affirming His Son, Jesus, He also commanded all of creation to hear Him. In other words, all of creation must obey the sound of Jesus' voice. This includes the wind and the waves; the sun, moon and stars. It includes the raising of the dead, too.

> The centurion answered and said, Lord, I am not worthy that thou shouldest

> come under my roof: but speak the
> word only, and my servant shall be
> healed. For I am a man under authority,
> having soldiers under me: and I say
> to this man, Go, and he goeth; and to
> another, Come, and he cometh; and to
> my servant, Do this, and he doeth it —
> Matthew 8:8-9 KJV.

What this centurion observed that we too need to know, is that all things in heaven, on earth and in hell are subject to the name of Jesus. The centurion stated that his authority as a Roman solder was limited but that Jesus' authority was limitless—that all that was required for things to fall into place was for Him to give the orders. Whatever He commanded to go, must go. Whatever He said to come, must come; and whenever He said to do this or that, it would do it. Jesus could give a command from Mongolia, and it would be obeyed in Seattle, Washington.

How To Access The Power in The Name of Jesus

> And His name, through faith in His name,
> has made this man strong, whom you
> see and know. Yes, the faith which
> comes through Him has given him this
> perfect soundness in the presence of
> you all — Acts 3:16 NKJV.

We access that power in His name by faith. It's faith in Jesus' name. And that faith is an imparted faith. It's faith that comes through Him or that is transmitted by Him. In other words, this faith that gives us perfect soundness in the presence of everyone is God's faith graciously transmitted into the one receiving the healing. It's the faith of the Son of God Himself — Galatians 2:20. Jesus is the means of His own mandates. This faith comes by hearing and hearing from the Word of God. And this is why we must feed on the Word of God at all times. As we feed upon His Word, faith from Him is imparted into our spirits — Ezekiel 2:2. And all that we would need in this life, including the perfect soundness of both soul and body is guaranteed by faith in His name. Therefore, continue to cultivate your faith by the constant study and meditation on the Word of God. This way, your faith will thrive and blossom beyond bounds. Living and walking in the revelation of the power of His name delivers swift answers to your prayers. Don't just call His name religiously. Call on it in faith, and watch the walls come tumbling down.

❧CHAPTER 6❧

THE LAW OF THE ABIDING WORD

I t's a beautiful thing to be constantly filled with God's Spirit. It's the surest way to a life of victory. And being filled with the Spirit comes from being filled with His Word. When our hearts are word-loaded, our lives spill over with praise, worship and thanksgiving. A precondition for asking and receiving is based on filling our hearts and minds with the Word of God.

> If ye abide in me, and my words abide in you, ye shall ask what ye will, and it shall be done unto you — John 15:7 KJV.

Abiding in Christ is a position we must maintain by faith and by practice. We may be alive in this world but we must continue to also breathe in oxygen to live in this world. Abiding in Christ requires that we continue to breathe in God's life through constant communion. His Word takes dominion over our lives but only to the degree that we abide in Him. His Word finds a resting place in us as we find a resting place in Him. The more we fellowship with Him, the more His life takes preeminence in us and the more His Word takes root in us. Abiding in Him is key to His

Word abiding in us. Have you ever wondered why at times you still feel very dry spiritually no matter how much of the Word you've studied? You know you've been reading it and studying it, but somehow, it's not reaching you in a way that's transforming you. Somehow, it feels like pouring water over concrete. The reason for this is you're missing the "abiding in Him part." It's the daily walk with Him part. How many times a day do we have to breathe in oxygen? Several thousand or maybe much more? Well, abiding in Him requires multiple moments of constant fellowship with God. Pausing throughout the day to acknowledge Him and show Him presence — Proverbs 3:5-6. This is how we actively live in Him and through Him. And as often as we do this, we create the necessary space for His Word to take root in us. I have discovered through personal experience that the more I spend time with God in prayer, the more His Word becomes real and alive in me. One feeds off of the other. This way, the more His Word finds a place in me, the more that Word saturates me and reigns over me. And as that word continues to rule and reign over me, my desires become more aligned to His. At this level, I find myself praying out His desires. In a sense, I'm making requests according to His will and according to the promptings of the Spirit of God. My heart filled with His Word guides my prayer requests, and a result, receives the needed answers.

CHAPTER 7

THE LAW OF SAVING LIVES & MAKING DISCIPLES

> You didn't choose me, but I chose you
> and appointed you so that you could
> go and produce fruit and so that your
> fruit could last. As a result, whatever
> you ask the Father in my name, he will
> give you — John 15:16 CEB.

Asking and receiving are directly connected to fruit-bearing. It's the fruit-bearing of saving lives and making disciples. If the church fully embraced this truth, it would revolutionize the way we live. If we lived this out, we would never again beg for bread or lack in anything. When Peter practiced this principle of the kingdom for the first time, it was the fish that came looking for him. When the lad with two fish and five loaves practiced it, he left with twelve baskets full from the leftovers. We'll understand the full meaning of life the moment this paradigm becomes a way of life—a life that's all about seeking and saving the lost and about making disciples. May this generation be the generation that will finally live out this mandate. The cure for all boredom lies in the call to save souls from hell. May this become our primary obsession. Imagine redefining evangelism. If every day became a soul-winning day where 99.9% of church folks engage all activities of life as soul-winning activities, imagine what that would do to impact whole communities in just one week. I'd like to post here a poem titled, "What if" from my book, "The Greatest Investment."

WHAT IF:

What if our thoughts were soul-winning thoughts?

What if our decisions were soul-winning decisions?

What if our actions were soul-winning actions?

What if our money was soul-winning money?

What if our assets were soul-winning assets?

What if every day was a soul-winning day?

What if our time was primarily a soul-winning time?

What if our jobs were seen as soul-winning jobs?

What if our dreams were soul-winning dreams?

What if our prayers were soul-winning prayers?

What if every platform was a soul-winning platform?

What if our very lifestyle was a soul-winning lifestyle?

What if all roads in life lead to the saving of a soul?

My prayer for you is that God's anointing upon your life first and foremost be a missional anointing. May the oil in your jar be poured into an endless number of empty vessels — Selah!

If the church took on the DNA of a soul winner, the world would feel the tremendous impact of the gospel of our Lord Jesus Christ in a matter of weeks.

HOW I DISCOVERED THE JACKPOT TO LIFE

In the reading and studying of the scriptures, I discovered the Jackpot to a life of unending success. I saw the secret. I discovered it in Luke fifteen. I saw what brought the most joy to God and His angels. I knew that if this one thing brought that much joy to God, it was worth sacrificing my very life for it. This was the one thing that caused the heavens to rejoice. It's the salvation of the soul of a sinner. I saw that very few things impressed God, but the saving of a single soul trumped them all. Saving souls moves God at His core. Since saving souls made all of God's angels party. In-fact, it's the only party they attend and I became committed to throwing as many of them as possible. If I could only bring that much joy to my Father's heart, mine would be a life worth living.

> "Suppose one of you had a hundred sheep and lost one. Wouldn't you leave the ninety-nine in the wilderness and go after the lost one until you found it? When found, you can be sure you would put it across your shoulders, rejoicing, and when you got home call

> in your friends and neighbors, saying,
> 'Celebrate with me! I've found my lost
> sheep!' Count on it—there's more joy in
> heaven over one sinner's rescued life
> than over ninety-nine good people in
> no need of rescue. Count on it—that's
> the kind of party God's angels throw
> every time one lost soul turns to God"
> — Luke 15:4-7, 10 MSG.

Yes, the harvesters get paid good wages. I knew that this was how I was going to terminate a life of perpetual poverty on earth as well as lay-up eternal treasures in the world to come. Saving souls is the key to the heart of the Father. And there isn't a better paymaster than God. He pays holistically — Genesis 24:1. Yes, He pays you in a grand style. And that pay increases as we disciple people to disciple others.

> The harvesters are paid good wages,
> and the fruit they harvest is people
> brought to eternal life. What joy awaits
> both the planter and the harvester alike!
> — John 4:36 NLT.

BOOK 4

THE EIGHT (8) PRAYER WATCHES OF THE BIBLE

HOW TO DEVELOP A STRONGER & CONSISTENT PRAYER LIFE

CHAPTER 1

DEFINING WHAT A PRAYER-WATCH IS

1) A watch is a stance in the spirit that places you in command of the future. Every watcher has a watch-tower or a watch post. And they tend to see things way ahead of time. Watching has to do with an alertness in the spirit that keeps you in the "know" of things — Mark 13:35-36 TPT. Watchmen are seers and custodians of the spirit world.

> I will stand upon my watch, and set me upon the tower, and will watch to see what he will say unto me, and what I shall answer when I am reproved —Habakkuk 2:1 KJV.

> For thus hath the Lord said unto me, Go, set a watchman, let him declare what he seeth — Isaiah 21:6 KJV.

2) I's a prayer life that positions you to flow in the frequency of the spirit.

Here, hearing from God comes as natural as hearing the voice of a parent.

> Continue in prayer, and watch in the same with thanksgiving — Colossians 4:2 KJV.

> Praying always with all prayer and supplication in the Spirit, and watching thereunto with all perseverance and supplication for all saints — Ephesians 6:18 KJV.

> I was in the Spirit on the Lord's day, and heard behind me a great voice, as of a trumpet — Revelation 1:10 KJV.

3) There is a special group of angels called the watchers. They're praying spirits and they come with a special prayer anointing. They've been trusted with an incredible amount of authority in the spirit. In the Book of Daniel, it shows that this group of angels take certain responsibilities upon their shoulder because of the trust they've earned with God. We see archangel Gabriel exercise such an authority over Zachariah's unbelief concerning the birth of his son, John. The Book of Hebrews calls it the consequences of disobeying the voice of an angel.

> I saw in the visions of my head upon my bed, and, behold, a watcher and an holy one came down from heaven — Daniel 4:13 KJV.

> "This sentence is by the decree of the angelic watchers. And the decision is a command of the holy ones ..." — Daniel 4:17 AMP.

4) Watching is a huge part of New Testament practice revealed both in the Gospels and Epistles

Apparently, the Bible has much to say about the watchman and what it means to watch. Jesus taught it in the gospels and the disciples practiced it in both Acts and the Epistles. We too, ought to practice it the same way. And if we do, we'll change the world for Jesus in no time. Introducing the body of Christ to all of the eight prayer watches of the Bible will introduce a wave of the Spirit of God, unheard of before. If we observe the prayer watch cycles, our glory banks would be filled, and, we could have it rain down for the next four decades nonstop.

> Watch ye therefore: for ye know not when the master of the house cometh, at even, or at midnight, or at the cockcrowing, or in the morning: Lest coming suddenly he find you sleeping. And what I say unto you I say unto all, Watch. — Mark 13:33-37 KJV.

> And in the fourth watch of the night Jesus went unto them, walking on the sea — Matthew 14:25 KJV.

> In stripes, in imprisonments, in tumults, in labours, in watchings, in fastings — 2 Corinthians 6:5 KJV.

> In weariness and painfulness, in watchings often, in hunger and thirst, in fastings often, in cold and nakedness — 2 Corinthians 11:27 KJV.

UNDERSTANDING THE NIGHT WATCHES

There is such a thing called the night watch or watches. And there are precisely four of them.

> The burden of Dumah. He calleth to me out of Seir, Watchman, what of the night? Watchman, what of the night
> — Isaiah 21:11 KJV.

> When I remember thee upon my bed, and meditate on thee in the night watches — Psalm 63:6 KJV.

> Mine eyes prevent the night watches, that I might meditate in thy word —Psalm 119:148 KJV.

₰CHAPTER 2₰

THE FOUR PRAYER WATCHES OF THE NIGHT

Watch ye therefore: for ye know not when the master of the house cometh, at even, or at midnight, or at the cockcrowing, or in the morning: Lest coming suddenly he find you sleeping — Mark 13:35 KJV.

Just so must you keep a look-out, for you do not know when the master of the house will come—it might be late evening, or midnight, or cock-crow, or early morning—otherwise he might come unexpectedly and find you sound asleep — Mark 13:35 PHILLIPS.

THE FIRST WATCH OF THE NIGHT (6PM TO 9PM) THE NEXT GENERATION IMPACT WATCH

The hearts of the people cry out to the Lord. Wall of Daughter Zion, let your

113

> tears run down like a river day and night.
> Give yourself no relief and your eyes no
> rest. Arise, cry out in the night from the
> first watch of the night. Pour out your
> heart like water before the Lord's pres-
> ence. Lift up your hands to Him for the
> lives of your children who are fainting
> from hunger on the corner of every
> street — Lamentations 2:18-19 HCSB.

The first night watch is also the beginning of all the watches. God places the foundation of all the prayer watches on impacting the next generation. Genesis chapter one defines time as starting from night into day or from the evening to the morning. **And God called the light Day, and the darkness he called Night. And the evening and the morning were the first day — Genesis 1:5 KJV.** The whole of the evening is <u>from 6pm to 6am</u>, while the whole of the day is <u>from 6am to 6pm</u> making it a twenty-four-hour cycle. The scriptures below show that the first watch is a night watch, and also the beginning of all the eight watches. In the KJV, it's called the "beginning of the watches." In the HCSB, it's called the "first watch of the night." In the AMP, it's called the "beginning of the night watches." Since time <u>starts at 6pm</u> in the evening, then, the first watch is <u>from 6pm to 9pm</u>.

THE NEXT GENERATION IMPACT WATCH

The first watch has to do with succession. It has to do with the continuity of the reign of God's kingdom in the earth. Isaiah speaks of a prolonging of His days through His seed. **Yet it pleased the Lord to bruise him; he hath**

put him to grief: when thou shalt make his soul an offering for sin, he shall see his seed, he shall prolong his days, and the pleasure of the Lord shall prosper in his hand —Isaiah 53:10 KJV. This extension of God's kingdom happens through succession—through the discipling of the next generation into a move of God. God is at the minimum, a three-generational God. He is the God of Abraham, Isaac and Jacob. The journey into Canaan did not happen with the first generation of people who came out of bondage—the Moses' generation, but rather it happened with the second—the Joshua generation. That next generation grew up amid the incomparable supernatural move of God. In other words, they were all raised and discipled in a move of God where miracles, signs and wonders were the culture of the day. This is the hunger our current generation of youngsters are fainting for on the corner of every street. They want to see Jesus in action. They want to see the Word of God in visible manifestation. They're tired of the dissonance that exists between the Bible and what they see in their lives. The first watch is therefore a prayer call to disciple the next generation into a move of God. Lamentations commands us to pour out of hearts like a flowing stream before the Lord. It commands us to pray unceasingly with our eyes full of tears until a move of God is birthed in and with the next generation, and the generation after them.

> Their heart cried unto the Lord, O wall of the daughter of Zion, let tears run down like a river day and night: give thyself no rest; let not the apple of thine eye cease. Arise, cry out in the night: in the beginning of the watches pour out thine heart like water before the face

115

of the Lord: lift up thy hands toward him for the life of thy young children, that faint for hunger in the top of every street — Lamentations 2:18-19 KJV.

Their hearts cried out to the Lord. "O wall of the Daughter of Zion, Let your tears run down like a river day and night; Give yourself no relief, Let your eyes have no rest. "Arise, cry aloud in the night, At the beginning of the night watches; Pour out your heart like water Before the presence of the Lord; Lift up your hands to Him For the life of your little ones Who are faint from hunger at the head of every street." Lamentations 2:18-19 AMP.

THE SECOND WATCH OF THE NIGHT (9PM TO 12PM) THE WATCH OF MEDITATIONS

When I remember thee upon my bed, and meditate on thee in the night watches — Psalm 63:6 KJV.

Mine eyes prevent the night watches, that I might meditate in thy word. Psalm 119:148 KJV.

The second watch of the night is a rich feast fellowship with God in His Word. It's prayer that's invoked by light—the light of God's Word. I remember one night in

Port Harcourt, River State, Nigeria where I taught on the resurrection of Christ. A praying anointing was invoked by reason of the light revealed from God's Word so that everyone spent the entire night in prayer. As you ponder over the Word, the light comes on and your heart burns within you as He speaks to you.

> And they said one to another, Did not our heart burn within us, while he talked with us by the way, and while he opened to us the scriptures? Luke 24:32 KJV.

Real Holy Ghost meditation sets the Word aflame in your heart, forcing your tongue to make life-altering decrees. The joy in the Holy Ghost bubbles up like wells of water. Here, you find yourself raptured in God's glory and caught up into the third heaven.

> My heart was hot within me, while I was musing the fire burned: then spake I with my tongue — Psalm 39:3 KJV.

THE THIRD WATCH OF THE NIGHT (12AM TO 3PM)
THE WATCH OF THE OPEN DOOR

> And at midnight Paul and Silas prayed, and sang praises unto God: and the prisoners heard them. And suddenly there was a great earthquake, so that the foundations of the prison were shaken: and immediately all the doors

were opened, and every one›s bands
were loosed. Acts 16:25-26 KJV.

A) The third watch of the night is the watch of the open
door. These open doors are very unusual and incredibly
uncommon. For the believer, it's freedom from all chains
and shackles of both soul and body. It's freedom from every
wound of the past; from every addiction of the present and
from all self-sabotaging patterns of the subconscious mind.
God's will for us is to walk in total freedom. It's freedom to
live your best life in Christ. This door opens up suddenly.
In order to free the world from all the power of Satan, we
must first walk in freedom.

> And it came to pass, that at midnight
> the Lord smote all the firstborn in the
> land of Egypt, from the firstborn of
> Pharaoh that sat on his throne unto the
> firstborn of the captive that was in the
> dungeon; and all the firstborn of cattle
> — Exodus 12:29 KJV.

B) The third watch is the watch of the open door from generational bondage into generational freedom. Take a good
look at your natural family's bloodline or lineage. What do
you see? Do you see the blessing or the curse at work? God
desires a generational paradigm shift in your family's lineage. He doesn't just want you free, He wants your entire
family free; including, the generations after them. He wants
to free your whole family tree. His desire is the salvation of
whole households. The children of Israel had lived in generational bondage for 430 years until the door to freedom
was opened in a single night. Suddenly, they were free.

C) The third watch is an open door from generational poverty into generational wealth. The same night of their freedom from bondage resulted in a night of great transfer of wealth. Suddenly, they became the wealthiest group of people on the planet.

> The Lord brought his people out of Egypt, loaded with silver and gold; and not one among the tribes of Israel even stumbled — Psalm 105:37 NLT.

D) The third watch of the night is also an open door into the gates of the city. It's a door of access for the spreading of the gospel, and for the influence of God's kingdom in the earth. It's a door of expansion and the unusual growth of the church.

> And Samson lay till midnight, and arose at midnight, and took the doors of the gate of the city, and the two posts, and went away with them, bar and all, and put them upon his shoulders, and carried them up to the top of an hill that is before Hebron — Judges 16:3 KJV.

E) The third watch is a watch for spiritual warfare and vengeance against all the works of the devil. Here, we pray against all the works of the devil militating against the spreading of the gospel and the influence of God's Word in the church. We pray against all doctrines of devils, and against his sway over the human mind.

> And Moses said, Thus saith the Lord, About midnight will I go out into the

> midst of Egypt: And all the firstborn in
> the land of Egypt shall die, from the
> first born of Pharaoh that sitteth upon
> his throne, even unto the firstborn of
> the maidservant that is behind the
> mill; and all the firstborn of beasts. And
> there shall be a great cry throughout
> all the land of Egypt, such as there was
> none like it, nor shall be like it any more
> — Exodus 11:4-6 KJV.

THE FOURTH WATCH OF THE NIGHT (3AM TO 6AM) OR THE EARLY MORNING WATCH.

A) The watch for the raw manifestation of unusual miracles.

> Between three and six o'clock in the
> morning, Jesus' followers were still
> in the boat. Jesus came to them. He
> was walking on the water—Matthew
> 14:25 ERV.

There's really something unusual about walking on water. It defies the laws of gravity. It's the imposition of a superior law completely outclassing and displacing natural law. As we observe this early morning watch, we will see unexplainable miracles that defy science and the natural order of things. This is that notable miracle that silenced the naysayers — Acts 4:16. The season of the greater works is upon us, and we are entering into it right now.

120

B) The Watch of His Presence

> O God, thou art my God; early will I
> seek thee: my soul thirsteth for thee,
> my flesh longeth for thee in a dry
> and thirsty land, where no water is;
> to see thy power and thy glory, so
> as I have seen thee in the sanctuary
> — Psalm 63:1-2 KJV.

This watch creates in us a deeper thirst for His presence—an insatiable hunger for Him. It's a longing for the revelation and manifestation of Jesus in power to an unbelieving world. Here, we yearn for Him just as the deer pants after the waters. We yearn to know Him and to make Him known. This watch is the watch of our personal communion with God.

> And in the morning, rising up a great
> while before day, he went out, and
> departed into a solitary place, and
> there prayed. And Simon and they that
> were with him followed after him. And
> when they had found him, they said
> unto him, All men seek for thee — Mark
> 1:35-37 KJV.

Who wants the whole world drawn to Jesus? Then, observe this Fourth watch of the night. And your soul will burn with a holy flame no force from hell can quench. In you will burn a divine jealousy for the honor of His name. On your lips, you will hear the cry of your heart sing: "Give me the nations or take me home; give me a rebirthing of Acts or take my life." Who's ready to enter here and never come out? The Spirit and the bride say come, Lord Jesus, come!

> And the Spirit and the bride say, Come.
> And let him that heareth say, Come.
> And let him that is athirst come. And
> whosoever will, let him take the water
> of life freely—Revelation 22:17 KJV.

C) The Fourth watch is the watch of the breakthrough.

It's the breaking forth of the dawn. It's the womb of the morning manifesting with all kinds of unusual breakthroughs. Here, the light of heaven invades and overshadows the darkness. This watch, if properly observed, will grant you access as a seer with tremendous power. This watch gives you power with God.

> And Jacob was left alone; and there
> wrestled a man with him until the
> breaking of the day. And he said, Thy
> name shall be called no more Jacob,
> but Israel: for as a prince hast thou
> power with God and with men, and hast
> prevailed — Genesis 32:24,28 KJV.

This watch places you in full command of the day. The seer who observes this watch downloads all the happenings and all activities of the day as if they've already taken place. He is not surprised because today existed in his yesterday. He's already ahead of the time.

⍥ CHAPTER 3 ⍦

THE FOUR PRAYER WATCHES OF THE DAY

J ust like the night watches, the day watches include four different kinds of watches. What's really unique about the day watches, however, is that the last three-day watches have to do with the spreading of the gospel.

1ST WATCH OF THE MORNING (6AM TO 9AM)
THE PRAISE & VICTORY WATCH

> And it came to pass, that in the morning watch the Lord looked unto the host of the Egyptians through the pillar of fire and of the cloud, and troubled the host of the Egyptians — Exodus 14:24 KJV.

This watch has to do with God's vengeance against all the enemies of your soul. Here, God steps in to fight for you. He takes personal responsibility for your life battles. He takes personal vengeance against them all. Like the armies of Pharaoh, He drowns them all into the sea of forgetfulness. God troubles your enemies for you, and neutralizes them so that no weapon formed against you can prosper.

> Ye shall not need to fight in this battle:
> set yourselves, stand ye still, and see
> the salvation of the Lord with you, O
> Judah and Jerusalem: fear not, nor be
> dismayed; to morrow go out against
> them: for the Lord will be with you —2
> Chronicles 20:17 KJV.

There are battles you will never have to fight because God fights for you. This watch is a watch where you celebrate your victory for winning. This is your praise-battle. It's your warfare worship. Here, in this watch, we spend ample time praising God and celebrating our victory through praise and worship. The first morning watch is a praise watch—it's a worship watch. It's a nonstop celebration of the finished work of Christ. Scriptures show that when we praise Him, He silences the enemy. Imagine such a battle strategy: "Appoint singers and let them praise Him in the beauty of holiness."

> And when they began to sing and to
> praise, the Lord set ambushments
> against the children of Ammon, Moab,
> and mount Seir, which were come
> against Judah; and they were smitten.
> 2 Chronicles 20:22 KJV.

In this first watch of the day, engage God with the weapon of your praise. Silence or extinguish the life out of your enemy. Choke the very life out of him. Take full command of your day. Your praise keeps you in charge.

> And it was so on the morrow, that Saul
> put the people in three companies; and

they came into the midst of the host in the morning watch, and slew the Ammonites until the heat of the day: and it came to pass, that they which remained were scattered, so that two of them were not left together — 1 Samuel 11:11 KJV.

The morning watch has been given to us to command the morning. That is, to set the order of the day. To tell the day how it must function and in what direction it must go. You're not at the mercy of the happenings of the day; rather, the day was designed to serve you in the way you would like it to go. How you begin your day is how you finish the day. The greater light to rule your day is at your disposal. If you get the day right, you're highly likely to get your night right. Come out from the secret place of prayer to command your day with vision; with victory; with a victor's mindset; with a prosperity mindset; with a champion's mindset; with a disease-free mindset—hallelujah!

Hast thou commanded the morning since thy days; and caused the dayspring to know his place?— Job 38:12 KJV.

2ND WATCH OF THE MORNING (9AM TO 12 NOON) THE CRUCIFIXION WATCH.

And it was the third hour, and they crucified him — Mark 15:25 KJV.

The second watch of the morning is the crucifixion watch. Jesus Christ, our Lord and Savior was crucified at an exact time—the third hour of the day or 9am in the morning. This watch is the watch of His Cross. All that His crucifixion, His death, His burial and His resurrection accomplished for us is included in this watch. The second watch of the morning is also the sixth watch of the day. Adding the numbers, you have the number of new beginnings. Our life in Christ began in the finished work of the cross. In this watch, we are to constantly pray over our complete and full redemptive rights in Christ Jesus. Psalms 103:1-5, spells out our redemptive rights. We are to see His cross as the fixed center of our lives, and we are to rehearse and rejoice over our legal right to all that the Father has bequeathed to us in His Son, Jesus Christ. We are to constantly make bold declarations of our legal inheritance in Christ. We experience more of His life at work in us as we make real our rights in Christ with our confession of faith.

> For these are not drunken, as ye suppose, seeing it is but the third hour of the day — Acts 2:15 KJV.

In addition, the second watch of the morning is a watch of fresh in-fillings of the Spirit. These waves of the fresh in-fillings of the Spirit of the Lord are predicated upon celebrating your rights in Christ. Let's form the habit of coming out in the mornings drunk in the Holy Spirit. It's time to live intoxicated. Life is far better under the Spirit's influence.

> Therefore being by the right hand of God exalted, and having received of the Father the promise of the Holy

> Ghost, he hath shed forth this, which
> ye now see and hear — Acts 2:33 KJV.

In other words, all that His Cross wrought for us culminates in the in-coming of the Holy Spirit into us. And now, He, the Holy Spirit, has made His home in you. "Christ in you" is the resultant gift of His own death and resurrection, and He lives in you through His Spirit. One more thing I need to point out is that the third hour is also intermediate between two time-frames. It's the intersection between the first and second watches of the morning. Here, in His Cross, Jesus, the victorious one defeats all our enemies and opens the way for us to enter into our inheritance. What a marvelous revelation!

3RD WATCH OF THE DAY (12 NOON TO 3PM)
THE WATCH OF THE SPREADING OF THE GOSPEL

The third watch of the morning is the watch of the spreading of the gospel of Christ. It's the sixth hour through to the ninth hour of the day or from twelve noon till three o'clock in the afternoon. During this time or watch, while Jesus hung on the cross, darkness fell over the land.

> And when the sixth hour was come,
> there was darkness over the whole
> land until the ninth hour. And at the
> ninth hour Jesus cried with a loud
> voice, saying, Eloi, Eloi, lama sabach-
> thani? which is, being interpreted, My
> God, my God, why hast thou forsaken
> me? — Mark 15:33-35 KJV.

This darkness is the darkness blinding the earth from seeing His work on the cross. It is the veil shrouding the earth in darkness — Isaiah 60:1-2. And yet, out of this darkness emerges the light of the glorious gospel of our Lord Jesus Christ — 2 Corinthians 4:4-6. We are to observe this watch praying for the swift spread of the gospel. We are to pray that the Word of the Lord run its course without demonic interference.

> Finally, brothers and sisters, pray continually for us that the word of the Lord will spread rapidly and be honored [triumphantly celebrated and glorified], just as it was with you — 2 Thessalonians 3:1 AMP.

As we observe this watch, the Lord of the harvest will open to us great and effectual doors for the gospel all around the world. In was during a third watch of the morning that God opened up the door of the gospel to the Gentile world. Peter went up the roof top to observe the third watch of the morning at precisely the sixth hour or twelve noon and fell into a trance or an open vision.

> On the morrow, as they went on their journey, and drew nigh unto the city, Peter went up upon the housetop to pray about the sixth hour: And he became very hungry, and would have eaten: but while they made ready, he fell into a trance, And saw heaven opened, and a certain vessel descending upon him, as it had been a great sheet knit at the four corners, and

let down to the earth: Wherein were all manner of four-footed beasts of the earth, and wild beasts, and creeping things, and fowls of the air. And there came a voice to him, Rise, Peter; kill, and eat. But Peter said, Not so, Lord; for I have never eaten any thing that is common or unclean. And the voice spake unto him again the second time, What God hath cleansed, that call not thou common. This was done thrice: and the vessel was received up again into heaven. Now while Peter doubted in himself what this vision which he had seen should mean, behold, the men which were sent from Cornelius had made enquiry for Simon's house, and stood before the gate, And called, and asked whether Simon, which was surnamed Peter, were lodged there. While Peter thought on the vision, the Spirit said unto him, Behold, three men seek thee. Arise therefore, and get thee down, and go with them, doubting nothing: for I have sent them. Then Peter went down to the men which were sent unto him from Cornelius; and said, Behold, I am he whom ye seek: what is the cause wherefore ye are come? And they said, Cornelius the centurion, a just man, and one that feareth God, and of good report among all the nation of the Jews, was warned from God by an holy angel to

> send for thee into his house, and to hear
> words of thee. Then called he them in,
> and lodged them. And on the morrow
> Peter went away with them, and certain
> brethren from Joppa accompanied him
> — Acts 10:9-23 KJV.

Here, Peter recounts his encounter with the dealings of God on how the door of the gospel opened up to the Gentile world. He tells them that it all happened during the third watch of the morning. I call this the Gospel-Watch. There has never been a more urgent time to preach it than now. Over four billion souls are at stake of eternal damnation. We should be all about the saving of the lost. Our entire lives need to be given to this one goal—seeking to save the lost.

> And the apostles and brethren that
> were in Judaea heard that the Gentiles
> had also received the word of God.
> And when Peter was come up to
> Jerusalem, they that were of the cir-
> cumcision contended with him, Saying,
> Thou wentest in to men uncircumcised,
> and didst eat with them. But Peter
> rehearsed the matter from the begin-
> ning, and expounded it by order unto
> them, saying, I was in the city of Joppa
> praying: and in a trance I saw a vision, A
> certain vessel descend, as it had been
> a great sheet, let down from heaven
> by four corners; and it came even to
> me: Upon the which when I had fas-
> tened mine eyes, I considered, and saw

fourfooted beasts of the earth, and wild beasts, and creeping things, and fowls of the air. And I heard a voice saying unto me, Arise, Peter; slay and eat. But I said, Not so, Lord: for nothing common or unclean hath at any time entered into my mouth. But the voice answered me again from heaven, What God hath cleansed, that call not thou common. And this was done three times: and all were drawn up again into heaven. And the Spirit bade me go with them, nothing doubting. Moreover these six brethren accompanied me, and we entered into the man's house: And he shewed us how he had seen an angel in his house, which stood and said unto him, Send men to Joppa, and call for Simon, whose surname is Peter; Who shall tell thee words, whereby thou and all thy house shall be saved. And as I began to speak, the Holy Ghost fell on them, as on us at the beginning. Then remembered I the word of the Lord, how that he said, John indeed baptized with water; but ye shall be baptized with the Holy Ghost. Forasmuch then as God gave them the like gift as he did unto us, who believed on the Lord Jesus Christ; what was I, that I could withstand God? When they heard these things, they held their peace, and glorified God, saying, Then hath God also to

> the Gentiles granted repentance unto
> life — Acts 11:1-10,12-18 KJV.

The sixth hour intersects between two time-frames. It falls between our redemptive rights (the celebration of all that His death and resurrection entails), and taking all that to a lost world. These rights we have in Christ were meant to be shared. We are to take these truths to a dying world. We are to tell them to see all that Christ accomplished for them in His Cross. How can we keep such a buffet to ourselves? Let's go and spread this great good news to the ends of the earth, hallelujah!

THE FOURTH WATCH OF THE DAY (3PM TO 6PM)
THE WATCH OF HOUSEHOLD SALVATIONS

During a fourth watch of the day or the ninth hour, which starts at 3pm in the afternoon, Cornelius, a Roman centurion, was praying and fasting when an angel from God spoke to him in a vision. He was instructed to send for Peter who would have words of godly wisdom for the salvation of his household.

> And Cornelius said, Four days ago I
> was fasting until this hour; and at the
> ninth hour I prayed in my house, and,
> behold, a man stood before me in
> bright clothing, And said, Cornelius, thy
> prayer is heard, and thine alms are had
> in remembrance in the sight of God
> Acts 10:30-31 KJV.

God wants our entire household to be saved. It's His ultimate will. It's divine design. Household salvation has been the plan from the beginning of time — Genesis 7:1. In this watch, our prayers should primarily be about our loved ones. There's an actual watch in the scriptures called the family watch.

> And I said to them, "Do not let the gates of Jerusalem be opened until the sun is hot; and while they stand guard, let them shut and bar the doors; and appoint guards from among the inhabitants of Jerusalem, one at his watch station and another in front of his own house." Nehemiah 7:3 NKJV.

Here, Nehemiah commands that the men set a watch over their own households. May God raise the men to watch over their own families in prayer. The Lord dedicated an entire watch to show how important our family members are to Him. The gospel does truly begin at Jerusalem before Judea, Samaria and the uttermost parts of the earth — Acts 1:8.

The fourth watch is also the watch for healing as a means to converting entire communities to Christ through the preaching of the gospel. As we continue to observe this watch, we will see more healings of this magnitude. These indisputable and irrefutable miracles will draw the lost to Jesus in multitudes.

> Now Peter and John went up together into the temple at the hour of prayer, being the ninth hour. And a certain man lame from his mother's womb

was carried, whom they laid daily at the gate of the temple which is called Beautiful, to ask alms of them that entered into the temple; Who seeing Peter and John about to go into the temple asked an alms. And Peter, fastening his eyes upon him with John, said, Look on us. And he gave heed unto them, expecting to receive something of them. Then Peter said, Silver and gold have I none; but such as I have give I thee: In the name of Jesus Christ of Nazareth rise up and walk. And he took him by the right hand, and lifted him up: and immediately his feet and ankle bones received strength. And he leaping up stood, and walked, and entered with them into the temple, walking, and leaping, and praising God. And all the people saw him walking and praising God — Acts 3:1-9 KJV.

Howbeit many of them which heard the word believed; and the number of the men was about five thousand — Acts 4:4 KJV.

⚚CHAPTER 4⚚

THE GLORY CIRCLE

These eight (8) "watches" form an endless cycle of prayer called the glory cycle. It works exactly the same as the water-cycle. As we continue to observe all eight watches of the Bible, like incense, our prayers and worship rise like water in gaseous form to fill the clouds of glory with the rain of His presence. In the flooding of the first world, the fountains of the deep were broken up and the windows of heaven opened to flood the earth with rain for forty days and forty nights. For the damned, it was a flood of destruction, but for the righteous, it was a flood of salvation. However, for this last great outpouring of the Spirit upon us, we will need to first fill our glory banks with the waters of our prayers. It's impossible to make a withdrawal where we have made no deposits. This is the mystery behind observing the prayer-watches. If we observe them accurately, we could have it rain for forty years nonstop. It all depends on how much rain we've deposited in our glory-bank. Will the Warrior Nation arise and take on this prayer responsibility? Will we arise and put on these prayer mantles? Will we join the angelic watchers of heaven led by our great intercessor, Jesus and labor for this unprecedented move of God as a clear path to reaching the world for Jesus?

CPSIA information can be obtained
at www.ICGtesting.com
Printed in the USA
FSHW010334140520

9 781545 679630